W9-APT-319

A LITERARY READER

African American WRITERS

nextext

Compiled by: Pamela E. Harkins, Northwestern University, Evanston, IL, and William J. Corrin, Northwestern University, Evanston, IL, and Evanston Township High School.

Cover photograph: Richard Wright, author of the classic novel *Native Son* and NAACP Springarn Medal winner. Courtesy of CORBIS.

Printed in the United States of America

ISBN 0-618-04813-8

1 2 3 4 5 6 7 — QKT — 06 05 04 03 02 01 00

Table of Contents

PART II: RHYTHMS OF BLACK LIFE

PART IV: FIGHTING ON TWO FRONTS: ON BEING BLACK AND AMERICAN

*Throughout the reader, vocabulary words appear in boldface
type and are footnoted. Specialized or technical words and phrases
appear in lightface type and are footnoted.*

Our
Foundations

Literacy and Liberation

BY FREDERICK DOUGLASS AND FRANCES E. W. HARPER

The earliest African-American writers were extraordinary individuals who overcame laws and customs aimed at preventing them from learning to read and write. Here two widely published, nineteenth-century authors write about the power of literacy. Frederick Douglass *(1817–1895) was a great champion of civil rights. Born a slave in Maryland, he escaped to freedom in his late teens and within three years became a lecturer in the abolitionist movement. Later he advised President Lincoln. In his autobiography,* Narrative of the Life of Frederick Douglass, an American Slave *(1845), Douglass recounts his experiences as a slave trying to learn to read.*

Unlike Douglass, Frances E. W. Harper (1825–1911) was born to free parents. She received an education in a school run by her uncle. An outspoken advocate for the end of slavery and of civil rights for blacks and women, Harper wrote about the central concerns of her life. In "Learning to Read," from Sketches of Southern Life *(1872), Harper describes how literacy empowered the people freed by the Civil War.*

Narrative of the Life of an American Slave
by Frederick Douglass

Very soon after I went to live with Mr. and Mrs. Auld, she very kindly **commenced**[1] to teach me the A, B, C. After I had learned this, she assisted me in learning to spell words of three or four letters. Just at this point of my progress, Mr. Auld found out what was going on, and at once forbade Mrs. Auld to instruct me further, telling her, among other things, that it was unlawful, as well as unsafe, to teach a slave to read. To use his own words, further, he said, "If you give a [slave] an inch, he will take an ell.[2] A [slave] should know nothing but to obey his master—to do as he is told to do. Learning would *spoil* the best [slave] in the world. Now," said he, "if you teach that [racial epithet] (speaking of myself) how to read, there would be no keeping him. It would forever unfit him to be a slave. He would at once become unmanageable and of no value to his master. As to himself, it could do him no good, but a great deal of harm. It would make him discontented and unhappy." These words sank deep into my heart, stirred up sentiments within that lay slumbering, and called into existence an entirely new train of thought. It was a new and special revelation, explaining dark and mysterious things, with which my youthful understanding had struggled, but struggled in vain. I now understood what had been to me a most perplexing difficulty—to wit, the white man's power to enslave the black man. It was a grand achievement, and I prized it highly. From that moment, I understood the pathway from slavery to freedom. It was just what I wanted, and I got it at a time when I the least expected it. Whilst I was saddened by the thought of losing the aid of my kind mistress, I was gladdened by the invaluable instruction which, by the

---

[1] **commenced**—began.

[2] an ell—more than a yard.

merest accident I had gained from my master. Though conscious of the difficulty of learning without a teacher, I set out with high hope, and a fixed purpose, at whatever cost of trouble, to learn how to read. The very decided manner with which he spoke, and strove to impress his wife with the evil consequences of giving me instruction, served to convince me that he was deeply sensible of the truths he was uttering. It gave me the best assurance that I might rely with the utmost confidence on the results which, he said, would flow from teaching me to read. What he most dreaded, that I most desired. What he most loved, that I most hated. That which to him was a great evil, to be carefully shunned, was to me a great good, to be diligently sought; and the argument which he so warmly urged, against my learning to read, only served to inspire me with a desire and determination to learn. In learning to read, I owe almost as much to the bitter opposition of my master, as to the kindly aid of my mistress. I acknowledge the benefit of both.

I lived in Master Hugh's family about seven years. During this time, I succeeded in learning to read and write. In accomplishing this, I was compelled to resort to various **stratagems**.[3] I had no regular teacher. My mistress, who had kindly commenced to instruct me, had, in compliance with the advice and direction of her husband, not only ceased to instruct, but had set her face against my being instructed by any one else. It is due, however, to my mistress to say of her, that she did not adopt this course of treatment immediately. She at first lacked the **depravity**[4] indispensable to shutting me up in mental darkness. It was at least necessary for her to have some training in the exercise of irresponsible power, to make her equal to the task of treating me as though I were a brute.

---

[3] **stratagems**—schemes.

[4] **depravity**—wickedness.

My mistress was, as I have said, a kind and tender-hearted woman; and in the simplicity of her soul she commenced, when I first went to live with her, to treat me as she supposed one human being ought to treat another. In entering upon the duties of a slaveholder, she did not seem to perceive that I sustained to her the relation of a mere **chattel**,[5] and that for her to treat me as a human being was not only wrong, but dangerously so. Slavery proved as injurious to her as it did to me. When I went there, she was a pious, warm, and tender-hearted woman. There was no sorrow or suffering for which she had not a tear. She had bread for the hungry, clothes for the naked, and comfort for every mourner that came within her reach. Slavery soon proved its ability to **divest**[6] her of these heavenly qualities. Under its influence, the tender heart became stone, and the lamblike disposition gave way to one of tiger-like fierceness. The first step in her downward course was in her ceasing to instruct me. She now commenced to practise her husband's **precepts**.[7] She finally became even more violent in her opposition than her husband himself. She was not satisfied with simply doing as well as he had commanded; she seemed anxious to do better. Nothing seemed to make her more angry than to see me with a newspaper. She seemed to think that here lay the danger. I have had her rush at me with a face made all up of fury and snatch from me a newspaper, in a manner that fully revealed her **apprehension**.[8] She was an apt woman; and a little experience soon demonstrated, to her satisfaction, that education and slavery were incompatible with each other.

From this time I was most narrowly watched. If I was in a separate room any considerable length of time,

---

[5] **chattel**—movable piece of personal property.

[6] **divest**—rid.

[7] **precepts**—rules.

[8] **apprehension**—uneasiness.

I was sure to be suspected of having a book, and was at once called to give an account of myself. All this, however, was too late. The first step had been taken. Mistress, in teaching me the alphabet, had given me the *inch* and no precaution could prevent me from taking the *ell*.

The plan which I adopted, and the one by which I was most successful, was that of making friends of all the little white boys whom I met in the street. As many of these as I could, I converted into teachers. With their kindly aid, obtained at different times and in different places, I finally succeeded in learning to read. When I was sent on errands, I always took my book with me, and by doing one part of my errand quickly, I found time to get a lesson before my return. I used also to carry bread with me, enough of which was always in the house, and to which I was always welcome; for I was much better off in this regard than many of the poor white children in our neighborhood. This bread I used to bestow upon the hungry little **urchins,**[9] who, in return, would give me that more valuable bread of knowledge. I am strongly tempted to give the names of two or three of those little boys, as a testimonial of the gratitude and affection I bear them; but **prudence**[10] forbids;—not that it would injure me, but it might embarrass them; for it is almost an unpardonable offence to teach slaves to read in this Christian country. It is enough to say of the dear little fellows, that they lived on Philpot Street, very near Durgin and Bailey's ship-yard. I used to talk this matter of slavery over with them. I would sometimes say to them, I wished I could be as free as they would be when they got to be men. "You will be free as soon as you are twenty-one, *but I am a slave for life*! Have not I as good a right to be free as you

---

[9] **urchins**—orphans; mischievous children.

[10] **prudence**—good judgment.

have?" These words used to trouble them; they would express for me the liveliest sympathy, and console me with the hope that something would occur by which I might be free.

I was now about twelve years old, and the thought of being *a slave for life* began to bear heavily upon my heart. Just about this time, I got hold of a book entitled "The Columbian Orator." Every opportunity I got, I used to read this book. Among much of other interesting matter, I found in it a dialogue between a master and his slave. The slave was represented as having run away from his master three times. The dialogue represented the conversation which took place between them, when the slave was retaken the third time. In this dialogue, the whole argument on behalf of slavery was brought forward by the master, all of which was disposed of by the slave. The slave was made to say some very smart as well as impressive things in reply to his master—things which had the desired though unexpected effect; for the conversation resulted in the voluntary **emancipation**[11] of the slave on the part of the master.

In the same book, I met with one of Sheridan's mighty speeches on and in behalf of Catholic emancipation. These were choice documents to me. I read them over and over again with **unabated**[12] interest. They gave tongue to interesting thoughts of my own soul, which had frequently flashed through my mind, and died away for want of utterance. The moral which I gained from the dialogue was the power of truth over the conscience of even a slaveholder. What I got from Sheridan was a bold **denunciation**[13] of slavery, and a powerful **vindication**[14] of human rights. The reading of these documents enabled me to utter my thoughts, and

---

[11] **emancipation**—release; freedom from slavery.

[12] **unabated**—unending, undying.

[13] **denunciation**—condemnation, criticism.

[14] **vindication**—justification.

to meet the arguments brought forward to sustain slavery; but while they relieved me of one difficulty, they brought on another even more painful than the one of which I was relieved. The more I read, the more I was led to **abhor**[15] and detest my enslavers. I could regard them in no other light than a band of successful robbers, who had left their homes, and gone to Africa, and stolen us from our homes, and in a strange land reduced us to slavery. I loathed them as being the meanest as well as the most wicked of men. As I read and contemplated the subject, behold! that very discontentment which Master Hugh had predicted would follow my learning to read had already come, to torment and sting my soul to unutterable anguish. As I writhed under it, I would at times feel that learning to read had been a curse rather than a blessing. It had given me a view of my wretched condition, without the remedy. It opened my eyes to the horrible pit, but to no ladder upon which to get out. In moments of agony, I envied my fellow-slaves for their stupidity. I have often wished myself a beast. I preferred the condition of the meanest reptile to my own. Any thing, no matter what, to get rid of thinking! It was this ever-lasting thinking of my condition that tormented me. There was no getting rid of it. It was pressed upon me by every object within sight or hearing, **animate**[16] or **inanimate**.[17] The silver trump of freedom had roused my soul to eternal wakefulness. Freedom now appeared, to disappear no more forever. It was heard in every sound, and seen in every thing. It was ever present to torment me with a sense of my wretched condition. I saw nothing without seeing it, I heard nothing without hearing it, and felt nothing without feeling it. It looked from every star, it smiled in every calm, breathed in every wind, and moved in every storm.

---

[15] **abhor**—hate.

[16] **animate**—living.

[17] **inanimate**—lifeless.

I often found myself regretting my own existence, and wishing myself dead; and but for the hope of being free, I have no doubt but that I should have killed myself, or done something for which I should have been killed. While in this state of mind, I was eager to hear any one speak of slavery. I was a ready listener. Every little while, I could hear something about the abolitionists. It was some time before I found what the word meant. It was always used in such connections as to make it an interesting word to me. If a slave ran away and succeeded in getting clear, or if a slave killed his master, set fire to a barn, or did any thing very wrong in the mind of a slaveholder, it was spoken of as the fruit of *abolition*. Hearing the word in this connection very often, I set about learning what it meant. The dictionary afforded me little or no help, I found it was "the act of abolishing"; but then I did not know what was to be abolished. Here I was perplexed. I did not dare to ask anyone about its meaning, for I was satisfied that it was something they wanted me to know very little about. After a patient waiting, I got one of our city papers, containing an account of the number of petitions from the north, praying for the abolition of slavery in the District of Columbia, and of the slave trade between the States. From this time I understood the words *abolition* and *abolitionist* and always drew near when that word was spoken, expecting to hear something of importance to myself and fellow-slaves. The light broke in upon me by degrees. I went one day down on the wharf of Mr. Waters; and seeing two Irishmen unloading a **scow**[18] of stone, I went, unasked, and helped them. When we had finished, one of them came to me and asked me if I were a slave. I told him I was. He asked, "Are ye a slave for life?" I told him that I was. The good Irishman seemed to be deeply affected by the statement. He said

---

[18] **scow**—flat-bottomed boat.

to the other that it was a pity so fine a little fellow as myself should be a slave for life. He said it was a shame to hold me. They both advised me to run away to the north; that I should find friends there, and that I should be free. I pretended not to be interested in what they said, and treated them as if I did not understand them; for I feared they might be treacherous. White men have been known to encourage slaves to escape, and then, to get the reward, catch them and return them to their masters. I was afraid that these seemingly good men might use me so; but I nevertheless remembered their advice, and from that time I resolved to run away. I looked forward to a time at which it would be safe for me to escape. I was too young to think of doing so immediately; besides, I wished to learn how to write, as I might have occasion to write my own pass. I consoled myself with the hope that I should one day find a good chance. Meanwhile I would learn to write.

The idea as to how I might learn to write was suggested to me by being in Durgin and Bailey's ship-yard, and frequently seeing the ship carpenters, after **hewing,**[19] and getting a piece of timber ready for use, write on the timber the name of that part of the ship for which it was intended. When a piece of timber was intended for the larboard[20] side, it would be marked thus—"L." When a piece was for the starboard side, it would be marked thus,— "S." A piece for the larboard side forward would be marked thus—"L. F." When a piece was for starboard side forward, it would be marked thus —"S. F." For larboard aft, it would be marked thus—"L. A." For starboard aft, it would be marked thus—"S. A." I soon learned the names of these letters, and for what they were intended when placed upon a piece of timber in the ship-yard.

---

[19] **hewing**—chopping, hacking with an axe.

[20] larboard—loading side of a ship.

I immediately commenced copying them, and in a short time was able to make the four letters named. After that, when I met with any boy who I knew could write, I would tell him I could write as well as he. The next word would be, "I don't believe you. Let me see you try it." I would then make the letters which I had been so fortunate as to learn, and ask him to beat that. In this way I got a good many lessons in writing, which it is quite possible I should never have gotten in any other way. During this time, my copy-book was the board fence, brick wall, and pavement; my pen and ink was a lump of chalk. With these, I learned mainly how to write. I then commenced and continued copying the Italics in *Webster's Spelling Book*, until I could make them all without looking on the book. By this time, my little Master Thomas had gone to school, and learned how to write, and had written over a number of copy-books. These had been brought home, and shown to some of our near neighbors, and then laid aside. My mistress used to go to class meeting at the Wilk Street meeting-house every Monday afternoon, and leave me to take care of the house. When left thus, I used to spend the time in writing in the spaces left in Master Thomas's copy-book, copying what he had written. I continued to do this until I could write a hand very similar to that of Master Thomas. Thus, after a long, tedious effort for years, I finally succeeded in learning how to write.

Learning to Read
by Frances E. W. Harper

Very soon the Yankee teachers
Came down and set up school;
But, oh! how the Rebs[21] did hate it,—
It was agin' their rule.

Our masters always tried to hide
Book learning from our eyes;
Knowledge didn't agree with slavery—
'Twould make us all too wise.

But some of us would try to steal
A little from the book,
And put the words together,
And learn by hook or crook.

I remember Uncle Caldwell,
Who took pot-liquor fat[22]
And greased the pages of his book,
And hid it in his hat.

And had his master ever seen
The leaves[23] upon his head,
He'd have thought them greasy papers,
But nothing to be read.

And there was Mr. Turner's Ben,
Who heard the children spell,
And picked the words right up by heart,
And learned to read 'em well.
Well, the Northern folks kept sending

---

[21] Rebs—Rebel or Confederate forces during the Civil War.

[22] pot-liquor fat—fatty broth from cooking meat and vegetables.

[23] leaves—book pages.

The Yankee teachers down;
And they stood right up and helped us,
Though Rebs did sneer and frown.

And, I longed to read my Bible,
For precious words it said;
But when I begun to learn it,
Folks just shook their heads,
And said there is no use trying,
Oh! Chloe,[24] you're too late;
But as I was rising sixty,
I had no time to wait.

So I got a pair of glasses,
And straight to work I went,
And never stopped till I could read
The hymns and **Testament.**[25]

Then I got a little cabin—
A place to call my own—
And I felt as independent
As the queen upon her throne.

---

[24] Chloe—poem's narrator.
[25] **Testament**—the Christian Bible.

QUESTIONS TO CONSIDER

1. When and how did Frederick Douglass come to understand that learning to read and write was important?

2. On page 17, Douglass writes of trying to discover what "the fruit of *abolition*" meant. How would you define the phrase?

3. What do Harper's lines "Oh! Chloe, you're too late; /But as I was rising sixty, /I had no time to wait" mean?

4. Why was literacy so important to both Frances E. W. Harper and Frederick Douglass?

from

Juneteenth

BY RALPH ELLISON

Ralph Ellison (1914–1994) is among the most important and influential American writers of the twentieth century. His first novel, Invisible Man *(1952), won the National Book Award and is considered to be one of the masterpieces of post-World War II American fiction.* Juneteenth, *Ellison's second novel, was a work-in-progress for forty years. Begun in 1954, it was not published until after Ellison's death.*

Juneteenth is the story of two men, the Reverend Alonzo Hickman, a jazz musician turned Baptist minister, and Senator Adam Sunraider, a self-named, race-baiting politician called Bliss when he was a boy. Ellison says Bliss was "a little boy of indefinite race who looks white and who, through a series of circumstances, comes to be reared by the Negro minister." After the Senator is shot by an assassin while giving a speech in the Senate, Reverend Hickman visits him in the hospital. There they retrace the course of their shared life. In the selection below, Bliss remembers a prayer meeting from the time he was a boy of ten. The participants were celebrating the day in the middle of June when news of Emancipation came to slaves in the South at the close of the Civil War. The narrator is Bliss (the Senator).

Still I see it after all the roving years and flickering scenes: Twin lecterns on opposite ends of the rostrum, behind one of which I stood on a wide box, leaning forward to grasp the lectern's edge. Back. Daddy Hickman at the other. Back to the first day of that week of celebration. Juneteenth. Hot, dusty. Hot with faces shining with sweat and the hair of the young dudes metallic with grease and straightening irons. Back to that? He was not so heavy then, but big with the quick energy of a fighting bull and still kept the battered silver trombone on top of the piano, where at the climax of a sermon he could reach for it and stand blowing tones that sounded like his own voice amplified; persuading, denouncing, rejoicing—moving beyond words back to the undifferentiated cry. In strange towns and cities the jazz musicians were always around him. Jazz. What was jazz and what religion back there? Ah yes, yes, I loved him. Everyone did, deep down. Like a great, kindly daddy bear along the streets, my hand lost in his huge paw. Carrying me on his shoulder so that I could touch the leaves of the trees as we passed. The true father, but black, black. Was he a **charlatan?**[1] Am I—or simply as resourceful in my fashion? Did he know himself, or care? Back to the problem of all that. Must I go back to the beginning when only he knows the start? . . .[2]

Juneteenth and him leaning across the lectern, resting there, looking into their faces with a great smile, and then looking over to me to make sure that I had not forgotten my part, winking his big red-rimmed eye at me. And the women looking back and forth from him to me with that bright, birdlike adoration in their faces; their heads cocked to one side. And him beginning:

---

[1] **charlatan**—fraud or quack who engages in grand, colorful schemes.

[2] These dots here and throughout this selection do not indicate something has been left out. Rather, they are Ellison's own marks to indicate a change in time from what Bliss remembers of the past to what he is thinking now.

On this God-given day, brothers and sisters, when we have come together to praise God and celebrate our oneness, our slipping off the chains, let's us begin this week of worship by taking a look at the ledger. Let us, on this day of deliverance, take a look at the figures writ on our bodies and on the living tablet of our heart. The Hebrew children have their Passover so that they can keep their history alive in their memories—so let us take one more page from their book and, on this great day of deliverance, on this day of emancipation, let's us tell ourselves our story. . . .

Pausing, grinning down . . . Nobody else is interested in it anyway, so let us enjoy it ourselves, yes, and learn from it.

And thank God for it. Now let's not be too solemn about it either, because this here's a happy occasion. Rev. Bliss over there is going to take the part of the younger generation, and I'll try to tell it as it's been told to me. Just look at him over there, he's ready and raring to go—because he knows that a true preacher is a kind of educator, and that we have got to know our story before we can truly understand God's blessings and how far we have still got to go. Now you've heard him, so you know that he can preach.

Amen! they all responded, and I looked preacher-faced into their shining eyes, preparing my piccolo[3] voice to support his baritone sound.

Amen is right, he said. So here we are, five thousand strong, come together on this day of celebration. Why? We just didn't happen. We're here and that is an undeniable fact—but how come we're here? How and why here in these woods that used to be such a long way from town? What about it, Rev. Bliss, is that a suitable question on which to start?

---

[3] piccolo—small flute that has a higher pitch than a standard flute.

God bless you, Rev. Hickman, I think that's just the place we have to start. We of the younger generation are still ignorant about these things. So please, sir, tell us just how we came to be here in our present condition and in this land. . . .[4]

Not back to that me, not to that six–seven-year-old ventriloquist's dummy dressed in a white evening suit. Not to that charlatan born—must I have no charity for me? . . . Not to that puppet with a memory like a piece of flypaper. . . .

Was it an act of God, Rev. Hickman, or an act of man? . . .

We came, amen, Rev. Bliss, sisters and brothers, as an act of God, but through—I said through—an act of cruel, ungodly man.

An act of Almighty God, *my treble echo sounded*, but through the hands of cruel man.

Amen, Rev. Bliss, that's how it happened. It was, as I understand it, a cruel calamity laced up with a blessing —or maybe a blessing laced up with a calamity. . . .

Laced up with a blessing, Rev. Hickman? We understand you partially because you have taught us that God's sword is a two-edged sword. But would you please tell us of the younger generation just why it was a blessing?

It was a blessing, brothers and sisters, because out of all the pain and the suffering, out of the night of storm, we found the Word[5] of God.

So here we found the Word. Amen, so now we are here. But where did we come from, Daddy Hickman?

We come here out of Africa, son; out of Africa.

Africa? Way over across the ocean? The black land? Where the elephants and monkeys and the lions and tigers are?

---

[4] Here and in the following passages, Ellison uses the dots to indicate a change in the speaker as the two men re-enact the old-time revival meeting.

[5] Word—the word of the Lord taken from the Bible.

Yes, Rev. Bliss, the jungle land. Some of us have fair skins like you, but out of Africa too.

Out of Africa truly, sir?

Out of the ravaged mama of the black man, son.

Lord, thou hast taken us out of Africa . . .

Amen, out of our familiar darkness. Africa. They brought us here from all over Africa, Rev. Bliss. And some were the sons and daughters of heathen kings . . .

Some were kings, Daddy Hickman? Have we of the younger generation heard you correctly? Some were kin to kings? Real kings?

Amen! I'm told that some were the sons and the daughters of kings . . .

. . . Of kings! . . .

And some were the sons and daughters of warriors . . .

. . . Of warriors . . .

Of fierce warriors. And some were the sons and daughters of farmers . . .

Of African farmers . . .

. . . And some of musicians . . .

. . . Musicians . . .

And some were the sons and daughters of weapon makers and smelters of brass and iron . . .

But didn't they have judges, Rev. Hickman? And weren't there any preachers of the word of God?

Some were judges, but none were preachers of the word of God, Rev. Bliss. For we come out of **heathen**[6] Africa . . .

Heathen Africa?

Out of heathen Africa. Let's tell this thing true; because the truth is the light.

And they brought us here in chains. . . .

In chains, son; in iron chains . . .

From half a world away, they brought us . . .

---

[6] **heathen**—not believing in the God of the Bible.

In chains and in boats that the history tells us weren't fit for pigs—because pigs cost too much money to be allowed to waste and die as we did. But they stole us and brought us in boats which I'm told could move like the swiftest birds of prey, and which filled the great trade winds with the stench of our dying and their crime. . . .

What a crime! Tell us why, Rev. Hickman. . . .

It was a crime, Rev. Bliss, brothers and sisters, like the fall of proud Lucifer from Paradise.[7]

But why, Daddy Hickman? You have taught us of the progressive younger generation to ask why. So we want to know how come it was a crime?

Because, Rev. Bliss, this was a country dedicated to the principles of Almighty God. That *Mayflower* boat that you hear so much about Thanksgiving Day was a *Christian* ship—amen! Yes, and those many-named floating coffins we came here in were Christian too. They had turned traitor to the God who set them free from Europe's tyrant kings. Because, God have mercy on them, no sooner than they got free enough to breathe themselves, they set out to bow us down. . . .

They made our Lord shed tears!

Amen! Rev. Bliss, amen. God must have wept like Jesus. Poor Jonah[8] went down into the belly of the whale, but compared to our journey his was like a trip to paradise on a silvery cloud.

Worse than old Jonah, Rev. Hickman?

Worse than Jonah slicked all over with whale puke and gasping on the shore. We went down into hell on those floating coffins and don't you youngsters forget it! Mothers and babies, men and women, the living and the dead and the dying—all chained together. And yet,

---

[7] Lucifer, the devil, was an angel who was sent out of heaven when he challenged God's authority.

[8] Jonah, a prophet from the Old Testament, was swallowed by a great whale and emerged unharmed three days later.

praise God, most of us arrived here in this land. The strongest came through. Thank God, and we arrived and that's why we're here today. Does that answer the question, Rev. Bliss?

Amen, Daddy Hickman, amen. But now the younger generation would like to know what they did to us when they got us here. What happened then?

They brought us up onto this land in chains . . .

. . . In chains . . .

. . . And they marched us into the swamps . . .

. . . Into the fever swamps, they marched us . . .

And they set us to work draining the swampland and toiling in the sun . . .

. . . They set us to toiling . . .

They took the white fleece of the cotton and the sweetness of the sugarcane and made them bitter and bloody with our toil. . . . And they treated us like one great unhuman animal without any face . . .

Without a *face*, Rev. Hickman?

Without personality, without names, Rev. Bliss, we were made into nobody and not even *Mister* Nobody either, just nobody. They left us without names. Without choice. Without the right to do or not to do, to be or not to be . . .

You mean without faces and without eyes? We were eyeless like Samson[9] in Gaza? Is that the way, Rev. Hickman?

Amen, Rev. Bliss, like bald-headed Samson before that nameless little lad like you came as the Good Book tells us and led him to the pillars whereupon the big house stood—Oh, you little black boys, and oh, you little brown girls, you're going to shake the building down! And then, oh, how you will build in the name of the Lord!

---

[9] Samson, a warrior from the Old Testament, possessed great physical strength, and, in battle with the Philistines, had his eyes gouged out.

Yes, Reverend Bliss, we were eyeless like unhappy Samson among the Philistines—and worse . . .

And WORSE?

Worse, Rev. Bliss, because they chopped us up into little bitty pieces like a farmer when he cuts up a potato. And they scattered us around the land. All the way from Kentucky to Florida; from Louisiana to Texas; from Missouri all the way down the great Mississippi to the Gulf. They scattered us around this land.

How now, Daddy Hickman? You speak in **parables**[10] which we of the younger generation don't clearly understand. How do you mean, they scattered us?

Like seed, Rev. Bliss; they scattered us just like a dope-fiend farmer planting a field with dragon teeth!

Tell us about it, Daddy Hickman.

They cut out our tongues . . .

. . . They left us speechless . . .

. . . They cut out our tongues . . .

. . . Lord, they left us without words . . .

. . . Amen! They scattered our tongues in this land like seed . . .

. . . And left us without language . . .

. . . They took away our talking drums . . .

. . . Drums that talked, Daddy Hickman? Tell us about those talking drums . . .

Drums that talked like a telegraph. Drums that could reach across the country like a church-bell sound. Drums that told the news almost before it happened! Drums that spoke with big voices like big men! Drums like a conscience and a deep heartbeat that knew right from wrong. Drums that told glad tidings! Drums that sent the news of trouble speeding home! Drums that told us *our* time and told us where we were . . .

Those were some drums, Rev. Hickman . . .

. . . Yes, and they took those drums away . . .

---

[10] **parables**—tales of truth; meaningful stories.

Away, amen! Away! And they took away our heathen dances . . .

. . . They left us drumless and they left us danceless . . .

Ah yes, they burnt up our talking drums and our dancing drums . . .

. . . Drums . . .

. . . And they scattered the ashes . . .

. . . Ah, aaaaaah! Eyeless, tongueless, drumless, danceless, ashes . . .

And a worse devastation was yet to come, Lord God!

Tell us, Revern Hickman. Blow on your righteous horn!

Ah, but Rev. Bliss, in those days we didn't have any horns . . .

No *horns?* Hear him!

And we had no songs . . .

. . . No songs . . .

. . . And we had no . . .

. . . Count it on your fingers, see what cruel man has done . . .

Amen, Rev. Bliss, lead them . . .

We were eyeless, tongueless, drumless, danceless, hornless, songless!

All true, Rev. Bliss. No eyes to see. No tongue to speak or taste. No drums to raise the spirits and wake up our memories. No dance to stir the rhythm that makes life move. No songs to give praise and prayers to God!

We were truly in the dark, my young brothers and sisters. Eyeless, earless, tongueless, drumless, danceless, songless, hornless, soundless . . .

And worse to come!

. . . And worse to come . . .

Tell us, Rev. Hickman. But not too fast so that we of the younger generation can gather up our strength to face it. So that we may listen and not become discouraged!

I said, Rev. Bliss, brothers and sisters, that they snatched us out of the loins of Africa. I said that they took us from our mammies and pappies and from our sisters and brothers. I said that they scattered us around this land . . .

. . . And we, let's count it again, brothers and sisters; let's add it up. Eyeless, tongueless, drumless, danceless, songless, hornless, soundless, sightless, dayless, nightless, wrongless, rightless, motherless, fatherless—scattered.

Yes, Rev. Bliss, they scattered us around like seed . . .

. . . Like seed . . .

. . . Like seed, that's been flung broadcast on unplowed ground . . .

Ho, chant it with me, my young brothers and sisters! Eyeless, tongueless, drumless, danceless, songless, horn-less, soundless, sightless, wrongless, rightless, motherless, fatherless, brotherless, sisterless, powerless . . .

Amen! But though they took us like a great black giant that had been chopped up into little pieces and the pieces buried; though they deprived us of our heritage among strange scenes in strange weather; divided and divided and divided us again like a gambler shuffling and cutting a deck of cards; although we were ground down, smashed into little pieces, spat upon, stamped upon, cursed and buried, and our memory of Africa ground down into powder and blown on the winds of foggy forgetfulness . . .

. . . Amen, Daddy Hickman! Abused and without shoes, pounded down and ground like grains of sand on the shores of the sea . . .

. . . Amen! And God—Count it, Rev. Bliss . . .

. . . Left eyeless, earless, noseless, throatless, teeth-less, tongueless, handless, feetless, armless, wrongless, rightless, harmless, drumless, danceless, songless, hornless, soundless, sightless, wrongless, rightless, motherless, fatherless, sisterless, brotherless, plowless, muleless, foodless, mindless—and Godless, Rev. Hickman, did you say Godless?

... At first, Rev. Bliss, he said, his trombone entering his voice, broad, somber and noble. At first. Ah, but though divided and scattered, ground down and battered into the earth like a spike being pounded by a ten-pound sledge, we were on the ground and in the earth and the earth was red and black like the earth of Africa. And as we moldered[11] underground we were mixed with this land. We liked it. It fitted us fine. It was in us and we were in it. And then—praise God—deep in the ground, deep in the womb of this land, we began to stir!

Praise God!

At last, Lord, at last.

Amen!

Oh the truth, Lord, it tastes so sweet!

What was it like then, Rev. Bliss? You read the scriptures, so tell us. Give us a word.

WE WERE LIKE THE VALLEY OF DRY BONES!

Amen. Like the Valley of Dry Bones in Ezekiel's dream.[12] Hoooh! We lay scattered in the ground for a long dry season. And the winds blew and the sun blazed down and the rains came and went and we were dead. Lord, we were dead! Except . . . Except . . .

... Except what, Rev. Hickman?

Except for one nerve left from our ear . . .

Listen to him!

And one nerve in the soles of our feet . . .

... Just watch me point it out, brothers and sisters . . .

Amen, Bliss, you point it out . . . and one nerve left from the throat . . .

... From our throat—right *here*!

... Teeth . . .

---

[11] moldered—grew moldy; decayed as a buried corpse.

[12] Ezekiel's dream—from the Old Testament, Ezekiel envisioned a valley of dry bones that came to life after receiving the Lord's spirit.

. . . From our teeth, one from all thirty-two of them . . .

. . . Tongue . . .

. . . Tongueless . . .

. . . And another nerve left from our heart . . .

. . . Yes, from our heart . . .

. . . And another left from our eyes and one from our hands and arms and legs and another from our stones . . .

Amen, hold it right there, Rev. Bliss . . .

. . . All stirring in the ground . . .

. . . Amen, stirring, and right there in the midst of all our death and buriedness, the voice of God spoke down the Word . . .

. . . Crying Do! I said, Do! Crying Doooo—

—these dry bones live?

He said: Son of Man . . . under the ground, ha! Heatless beneath the roots of plants and trees . . . Son of Man, do . . .

I said, Do . . .

. . . I said Do, Son of Man, Doooooo!—

—these dry bones live?

Amen! And we heard and rose up. Because in all their blasting they could not blast away one solitary vibration of God's true word. . . . We heard it down among the roots and among the rocks. We heard it in the sand and in the clay. We heard it in the falling rain and in the rising sun. On the high ground and in the gullies. We heard it lying moldering and corrupted in the earth. We heard it sounding like a bugle call to wake up the dead. Crying, Doooooo! Ay, do these dry bones live!

And did our dry bones live, Daddy Hickman?

Ah, we sprang together and walked around. All clacking together and clicking into place. All moving in time! Do! I said, Dooooo——these dry bones live!

And now strutting in my white tails, across the platform, filled with the power almost to dancing.

Shouting, Amen, Daddy Hickman, is this the way we walked?

Oh we walked through Jerusalem, just like John— That's it, Rev. Bliss, walk! Show them how we walked!

Was this the way?

That's the way. Now walk on back. Lift your knees! Swing your arms! Make your coattails fly! Walk! And him strutting me three times around the pulpit across the platform and back. Ah, yes! And then his voice deep and exultant: And if they ask you in the city why we praise the Lord with bass drums and brass trombones tell them we were rebirthed dancing, we were rebirthed crying affirmation of the Word, quickening our **transcended**[13] flesh.

Amen!

Oh, Rev. Bliss, we stamped our feet at the trumpet's sound and we clapped our hands, ah, in joy! And we moved, yes, together in a dance, amen! Because we had received a new song in a new land and been resurrected by the Word and Will of God!

Amen! . . .

. . . We were rebirthed from the earth of this land and **revivified**[14] by the Word. So now we had a new language and a brand-new song to put flesh on our bones . . .

New teeth, new tongue, new word, new song!

We had a new name and a new blood, and we had a new task . . .

Tell us about it, Reveren Hickman . . .

We had to take the Word for bread and meat. We had to take the Word for food and shelter. We had to use the Word as a rock to build up a whole new nation, 'cause to tell it true, we were born again in chains of steel. Yes, and chains of ignorance. And all we knew was the spirit of the Word. We had no schools. We owned no tools, no cabins, no churches, not even our own bodies.

---

[13] **transcended**—more than human.

[14] **revivified**—restored to life.

We were chained, young brothers, in steel. We were chained, young sisters, in ignorance. We were school-less, toolless, cabinless—owned . . .

Amen, Reveren Bliss. We were owned and faced with the awe-inspiring labor of transforming God's Word into a lantern so that in the darkness we'd know where we were. Oh, God hasn't been easy with us because He always plans for the loooong haul. He's looking far ahead and this time He wants a well-tested people to work his will. He wants some sharp-eyed, quick-minded, generous-hearted people to give names to the things of this world and to its values. He's tired of **untempered**[15] tools and half-blind masons! Therefore, He's going to keep on testing us against the rocks and in the fires. He's going to plunge us into the ice-cold water. And each time we come out we'll be blue and as tough as cold-blue steel! Ah yes! He means for us to be a new kind of human. Maybe we won't be that people but we'll be a part of that people, we'll be an element in them, amen! He wants us limber as willow switches and he wants us tough as whip leather, so that when we have to bend, we can bend and snap back into place. He's going to throw bolts of lightning to blast us so that we'll have good footwork and lightning-fast minds. He'll drive us hither and yon around this land and make us run the **gauntlet**[16] of hard times and tribulations, mis-understanding and abuse. And some will pity you and some will despise you. And some will try to use you and change you. And some will deny you and try to deal you out of the game. And sometimes you'll feel so bad that you'll wish you could die. But it's all the pressure of God. He's giving you a will and He wants you to use it. He's giving you brains and he wants you to train them lean and hard so that you can overcome all the obsta-cles. Educate your minds! Make do with what *you* have

---

[15] **untempered**—poorly constructed; unhardened metal.

[16] **gauntlet**—challenge; contest of strength.

so as to get what you need! Learn to look at what *you* see and not what somebody tells you is true. Pay lip service to Caesar[17] if you have to, but put your trust in God. Because nobody has a patent on truth or a copyright on the best way to live and serve Almighty God. Learn from what we've lived. Remember that when the labor's back-breaking and the bossman's mean our singing can lift us up. That it can strengthen us and make his meanness but the flyspeck irritation of an empty man. Roll with the blow like ole Jack Johnson.[18] Dance on out of his way like Williams and Walker.[19] Keep to the rhythm and you'll keep to life. God's time is long; and all short-haul horses shall be like horses on a merry-go-round. Keep, keep, keep to the rhythm and you won't get weary. Keep to the rhythm and you won't get lost. We're handicapped, amen! Because the Lord wants us strong! We started out with nothing but the Word—just like the others, but they've forgot it. . . . We worked and stood up under hard times and tribulations. We learned patience and to understand Job. Of all the animals, man's the only one not born knowing almost everything he'll ever know. It takes him longer than an elephant to grow up because God didn't mean him to leap to any conclusions, for God Himself is in the very process of things. We learned that all blessings come mixed with sorrow and all hardships have a streak of laughter. Life is a streak-a-lean—a streak-a fat. Ha, yes! We learned to bounce back and to disregard the prizes of fools. And we must keep on learning. Let them have their fun. Even let them eat hummingbirds' wings and tell you it's too good for you. —Grits and greens

---

[17] Caesar—powerful ancient Roman emperor. This is a reference to Jesus's answer regarding taxes: "Give to Caesar what is Caesar's but give to God, what is God's."

[18] Jack Johnson—the first black heavyweight boxing champion in the United States.

[19] Williams and Walker—Bert Williams and George Walker were famous turn-of-the-century African-American entertainers.

don't turn to ashes in anybody's mouth—how about it, Rev. Eatmore? Amen? Amen! Let everybody say amen. Grits and greens are humble but they make you strong and when the right folks get together to share them they can taste like **ambrosia**.[20] So draw, so let us draw on our own wells of strength.

Ah yes, so we were reborn, Rev. Bliss. They still had us harnessed, we were still laboring in the fields, but we had a secret and we had a new rhythm . . .

So tell us about this rhythm, Reveren Hickman.

They had us bound but we had our kind of time, Rev. Bliss. They were on a merry-go-round that they couldn't control but we learned to beat time from the seasons. We learned to make this land and this light and darkness and this weather and their labor fit us like a suit of new underwear. With our new rhythm, amen, but we weren't free and they still kept dividing us. There's many a thousand gone down the river. Mamma sold from papa and chillun sold from both. Beaten and abused and without shoes. But we had the Word, now, Rev. Bliss, along with the rhythm. They couldn't divide us now. Because anywhere they dragged us we throbbed in time together. If we got a chance to sing, we sang the same song. If we got a chance to dance, we beat back hard times and tribulations with the clap of our hands and the beat of our feet, and it was the same dance. Oh, they come out here sometimes to laugh at our way of praising God. They can laugh but they can't deny us. They can curse and kill us but they can't destroy us all. This land is ours because we come out of it, we bled in it, our tears watered it, we fertilized it with our dead. So the more of us they destroy the more it becomes filled with the spirit of our **redemption**.[21] They laugh but we know who we are and where we are,

---

[20] **ambrosia**—sweet, heavenly dessert.

[21] **redemption**—freedom from captivity; release.

but they keep on coming in their millions and they don't know and can't get together.

But tell us, how do we know who we are, Daddy Hickman?

We know where we are by the way we walk. We know where we are by the way we talk. We know where we are by the way we sing. We know where we are by the way we dance. We know where we are by the way we praise the Lord on high. We know where we are because we hear a different tune in our minds and in our hearts. We know who we are because when we make the beat of our rhythm to shape our day the whole land says, Amen! It smiles, Rev. Bliss, and it moves to our time! Don't be ashamed, my brothers! Don't be cowed. Don't throw what you have away! Continue! Remember! Believe! Trust the inner beat that tells us who we are. Trust God and trust life and trust this land that is you! Never mind the laughers, the scoffers—they come around because they can't help themselves. They can deny you but not your sense of life. They hate you because whenever they look into a mirror they fill up with bitter **gall.**[22] So forget them, and most of all don't deny yourselves. They're tied by the short hairs to a runaway merry-go-round. They make life a business of struggle and fret, fret and struggle. See who you can hate; see what you can get. But you just keep on inching along like an old inchworm. If you put one and one and one together soon they'll make a million too. There's been a heap of Juneteenths before this one and I tell you there'll be a heap more before we're truly free! Yes! But keep to the rhythm, just keep to the rhythm and keep to the way. Man's plans are but a joke to God. Let those who will despise you, but remember deep down inside yourself that the life we have to lead is but a preparation for other things, it's a discipline, Reveren Bliss, sisters

---

[22] **gall**—bile, a body fluid secreted by the liver to aid digestion; a bitterness of feeling.

and brothers; a discipline through which we may see that which the others are too self-blinded to see. Time will come round when we'll have to be their eyes; time will swing and turn back around. I tell you, time shall swing and spiral back around. . . .

QUESTIONS TO CONSIDER

1. What are some of the lessons that Reverend Hickman and his elders are attempting to pass on to the younger generation?

2. How did scripture and the Word of the Lord enable African-American people to survive slavery?

3. How does the preacher's sermon function as a powerful means of storytelling?

Rising from the Past

BY JAMES WELDON JOHNSON,
SABAH AS-SABAH, AND
J. ROSAMUND JOHNSON

*Two poems and a traditional spiritual celebrate ancestors and
the traditions of African-American heritage. In "The Creation,"
novelist and poet James Weldon Johnson (1871–1938) uses sermon-
like language to retell the story of the earth's formation. In "Jubilee,"
contemporary poet Sabah As-Sabah (1963–1995) links the continuing African-American odyssey to the history of plantation life and
the struggle against slavery. He recalls several nineteenth-century
literary and political figures who wrote about the abolition of slavery—
Harriet (Wilson), Benjamin (Banneker), Frederick (Douglass),
Alexander (Dumas), and "deceased sojourners" (Sojourner Truth
and others). In the spiritual "Lift Ev'ry Voice and Sing," recorded
by James Weldon Johnson and his brother John Rosamund Johnson,
voices are raised in rejoicing. The poem was written to honor
President Lincoln's birthday and the emancipation he represents.*

The Creation

BY JAMES WELDON JOHNSON

And God stepped out on space,
And He looked around and said,
"I'm lonely—
I'll make me a world."

And far as the eye of God could see
Darkness covered everything,
Blacker than a hundred midnights
Down in a cypress swamp.

Then God smiled,
And the light broke,
And the darkness rolled up on one side,
And the light stood shining on the other,
And God said, *"That's good!"*

Then God reached out and took the light in His hands,
And God rolled the light around in His hands,
Until He made the sun;
And He set that sun a-blazing in the heavens.
And the light that was left from making the sun
Got gathered up in a shining ball
And flung against the darkness,
Spangling the night with the moon and stars.
Then down between
The darkness and the light
He hurled the world;
And God said, *"That's good!"*

Then God himself stepped down—
And the sun was on His right hand,
And the moon was on His left;
The stars were clustered about His head,

And the earth was under His feet.
And God walked, and where He **trod**[1]
His footsteps hollowed the valleys out
And bulged the mountains up.

Then He stopped and looked and saw
That the earth was hot and barren.
So God stepped over to the edge of the world
And He spat out the seven seas;
He batted His eyes, and the lightnings flashed;
He clapped His hands, and the thunders rolled;
And the waters above the earth came down,
The cooling waters came down.

Then the green grass sprouted,
And the little red flowers blossomed,
The pine-tree pointed his finger to the sky,
And the oak spread out his arms;
The lakes cuddled down in the hollows of the ground,
And the rivers ran down to the sea;
And God smiled again,
And the rainbow appeared,
And curled itself around His shoulder.

Then God raised His arm and He waved His hand
Over the sea and over the land,
And He said, *"Bring forth! Bring forth!"*
And quicker than God could drop His hand,
Fishes and fowls
And beast and birds
Swam the rivers and the seas,
Roamed the forests and the woods,
And split the air with their wings,
And God said, *"That's good!"*

---

[1] **trod**—stepped.

Then God walked around
And God looked around
On all that He had made.
He looked at His sun,
And He looked at His moon,
And He looked at His little stars;
He looked on His world
With all its living things,
And God said, *"I'm lonely still."*

Then God sat down
On the side of a hill where He could think;
By a deep, wide river He sat down;
With His head in His hands,
God thought and thought,
Till He thought, *"I'll make me a man!"*

Up from the bed of the river
God scooped the clay,
And by the bank of the river
He kneeled Him down;
And there the great God Almighty,
Who lit the sun and fixed it in the sky,
Who flung the stars to the most far corner of the night,
Who rounded the earth in the middle of His hand—
This Great God,
Like a mammy bending over her baby,
Kneeled down in the dust
Toiling[2] over a lump of clay
Till He shaped it in His own image;

Then into it He blew the breath of life,
And man became a living soul.
Amen. Amen.

---

[2] **toiling**—working.

Jubilee

BY SABAH AS-SABAH

I feel warm
in the muds of Louisiana
heating up my swollen ankles
as I make my way through the dead flies and agitated
grasshoppers
past deceased sojourners
who enrich my journey
with stories of rabbits and bears
I catch the wind in hair too heavy with history to move
and smell
the **rank**[3] of honeysuckle and burning flesh
rolling underground,
I move to higher ground and run alongside the railroad
Feelin' the strength of my toes and the age of my oak
I take legendary leaps over plantations
"one step, two step, three step more"
Flying past the cotton fields and gliding over the
    corn fields
I call my children's names
Come Harriet
Come Benjamin
Come Frederick
Come Alexander
I sing my song of Jubilee
sharing secrets with the sun
and shoutin' praises with the moon.

---

[3] **rank**—bad odor.

Lift Ev'ry Voice and Sing

BY JAMES W. JOHNSON AND
J. ROSAMUND JOHNSON

Lift ev'ry voice and sing,
Till earth and heaven ring,
Ring with the harmonies of Liberty;
Let our rejoicing rise
High as the list'ning skies,
Let it resound loud as the rolling sea.
Sing a song full of the faith that the dark past
   has taught us
Sing a song full of the hope that the present has
   brought us
Facing the rising sun of our new day begun,
Let us march on till victory is won.

Stony the road we trod,
Bitter the chast'ning rod,[4]
Felt in the days when hope unborn had died;
Yet with a steady beat,
Have not our weary feet
Come to the place for which our fathers sighed?
We have come over a way that with tears has
   been watered
We have come, treading our path thro' the
   blood of the slaughtered,
Out from the gloomy past, till now we stand at last
Where the white gleam of our bright star is cast.

God of our weary years,
God of our silent tears,
Thou who hast brought us thus far on the way;

---

[4] chast'ning rod—whip or switch used to punish.

Thou who hast by Thy might,
Led us into the light,
Keep us forever in the path, we pray.

Lest our feet stray from the places, our God,
     where we met Thee,
Lest our hearts, drunk with the wine of the
     world, we forget thee;
Shadowed beneath Thy hand, may we forever stand,
True to our God, true to our native land.

QUESTIONS TO CONSIDER

1. What is significant about James Weldon Johnson's use of language in "The Creation"? How does it add to or take away from the reading?

2. Why do you think As-Sabah chose the title "Jubilee" for his poem?

3. In "Lift Ev'ry Voice and Sing," what victory is referred to by the lines, "Facing the rising sun of our new day begun,/Let us march on until victory is won"?

4. What lines or terms in the selections link them to the past? Why is the past important?

5. What lessons might these selections offer about the future of the black experience? Use examples from the poems in your answer.

Treasures of Time

BY FLORIDA RUFFIN RIDLEY

The continual efforts of Florida Ruffin Ridley (1861–1943) to improve the status of blacks and women were a fundamental part of her life. She was active in both local and national civil rights organizations. Although Ridley was involved earlier in her life in the editing and publishing of Women's Era, *a journal for black women, her own short stories and essays did not begin to be published until the 1920s, most often in the Harlem Renaissance journals* Saturday Evening Quill *and* Opportunity. *The essay included here, which appeared in a 1928* Saturday Evening Quill, *documents the history of an upper middle-class black family back to its African ancestor.*

I have dragged the heavy old box from under the kitchenette shelf; it is one of those strongly built boxes which praise the honest workmanship of a former century and which, with other like furnishings, has accompanied those transitions from farm house to city house, from city house to city apartment.

Here, under the kitchenette shelf, it is wholly out of keeping with electric stove and refrigerator, being as large as one and much larger than the other. Besides, the unavoidable bruising of shins against its corners is becoming monotonously irritating, and the temptation to crowd into it all sorts of things that happen to be in the way has led to many unfortunate results—as when a bag of apples, stuffed hastily in a corner, was forgotten and left to decay, the stain almost **obliterating**[1] the written words of a most charming love letter of the fifties.

So today the first step in the discard is being taken, a sorting of the treasures in the box preparatory to putting them into other and less clumsy containers.

What should be sacrificed and what preserved? It is impossible to deny the charm of things that connect with the past; and **rifling**[2] old boxes for letters, documents, and pictures to meet the demand and interest, has become such a general pastime, one wonders if there be anything worthwhile that has not been already revealed. At least there would seem to be few phases of early American life that have not been wholly or partly disclosed through the contents of such boxes as these: we have been given more or less vivid pictures of life in old New England and of pioneer life in the Middle West; we have been led to know the Dutch Master and the Puritan Preacher and to follow the Covered Wagon; but here is a Treasure Trove that is unique in its way, not especially because it represents the hundred-years' accumulation of an American family (in this it can be many times duplicated), but because its old deeds and Bibles, its letters and receipts, its pictures and pamphlets are the records of a Boston Negro family, a family justifiably[3] but modestly making its claim as "Bostonian" because of three generations (through the maternal line)

---

[1] **obliterating**—blotting out.

[2] **rifling**—rummaging through; searching.

[3] justifiably—fairly; with good reason.

born in Boston and free in Massachusetts; a family which has its known beginning when a captured African escaped from a trading vessel in the port of New Bedford, fled to the woods around what is now known as Taunton, and took an Indian squaw as his wife; a family one line of which was continued in that neighborhood through a venturing Negro from Martinique, and of which one descendant left the farming and basket-making of his forebears, settled in Boston, and married an English girl fresh from Cornwall; a family vividly representing the American "melting pot," that "melting pot" to which, in every section of this country, the Negro is largely contributing.

Through these varying phases of family life, the contents of this chest have traveled—phases and events which **antedate**[4] the box itself—and now to meet the demands of the new generation and of the new times for more room, this sorting and filing is being done.

Old letters naturally comprise the bulk of the contents; some folded and sealed with postage to be paid at the door, all written on cheap and homely paper. Most of them are given over to family affairs, but many make astonishing yet **unaffected**[5] references to persons whose names have a place in American history.

Here, for instance, is a letter of comparatively recent date—November 28, 1862—which records the Thanksgiving Day when Governor Andrew came down Beacon Hill to dine with colored people in one of their homes on Phillips Street. An extract follows:

"We had a nice Thanksgiving dinner at home . . . turkey, oysters, plum pudding and Apple Jack. . . . Mr. H—came over in the afternoon to invite me to his home at five o'clock. . . . I was seated next to Governor Andrew and was talking with him a good part of the

---

[4] **antedate**—predate, came before.

[5] **unaffected**—natural.

time. The Governor was very **affable**[6] and sat through all the courses from 5½ to past 8 o'clock. The Secretary left about 7 o'clock to take his train."

Here is another letter in the neat, clear and fine handwriting of Frederick Douglass, sent to a member of the family appointed as a Massachusetts Justice. Douglass's letter begins, "May It Please Your Honor. . . ." Here is another letter from Douglass sent from his office as Recorder of Deeds for the District of Columbia. To quote from it:

"Soon after entering upon the duties of his office, I was asked by Mr. Blaine, Secretary of State, to name certain colored men to be sent abroad. They were to be such as in my judgment would reflect credit upon themselves, the Country and the Republican Party. I asked him to give me time. The next day I sent him a letter with five names, and yours was first on the list."

Here is another, a family letter written the day after the assassination of President Lincoln, a simple letter, but significant as presenting a true picture of what Negroes in Boston were doing and thinking at that time.

Here are old Bibles with more than a century of family records; here are deeds and mortgage notes, and here is a memorandum of a grant of land to a collateral line;[7] the grant made in 1786 by the Great and General Court of Massachusetts and recorded in the County Court of Taunton, near which city the land is located. This gift of the State was made in recognition of the services in the Revolutionary War of the receiver, who had been a Massachusetts slave and who was granted his freedom at the same time.

Here is a copy of the will of a forebear upon the paternal side, a document **probated**[8] in the city of

---

[6] **affable**—good-natured.

[7] collateral line—descendants from the same ancestors but from a different family line.

[8] **probated**—proven to be genuine.

Richmond, Virginia, in 1839, and which lists and **apportions**[9] to the family of the maker houses, money and furniture accumulated by a Virginia Negro at the end of the seventeenth century. Here are letters relating to the execution of this will and to the use of the money by one of the heirs, who was actively interested in the early Liberian Colonization Scheme.[10] With these is a passport, issued in 1852, to one of the descendants of this old Virginian, a paper which gave him the privilege "as a free person of color," of moving about under certain restrictions, in his native city of Richmond.

In **light relief**[11] to these documents of civic and legal bearing are those of social importance and significance. Here are bills and receipts for food, for furniture, for medical treatment, all indicating economic status; here are daguerreotypes[12] and souvenirs, wedding invitations and calling cards. Among the souvenirs are dried and brittle relics of the old basket-work done years ago by the Taunton branch of the family, who were Yankee farmers during the summer and straw weavers during the winter; who used to send their cranberries into Boston for Thanksgiving and leave the planting of the June peas until after Anniversary-Week meetings in Boston.

The calling cards and invitations are combinations of the town branch of the family—glazed stationery seems to have been the mode in the Victorian Era, for this highly polished Silver Wedding Anniversary card was put out by "Loring" of high Boston repute. It carries the announcement of the twenty-fifth anniversary of the marriage of a Boston couple living on the then very desirable Shawmut Avenue, and the date of the affair is

---

[9] **apportions**—distributes; gives parts, usually of an estate.

[10] Liberian Colonization Scheme—plan for free American blacks to settle in the African country Liberia.

[11] **light relief**—in comparison.

[12] daguerreotypes—early photographs made on chemically treated metal or glass.

February 22, 1869. There are records that this Negro family further voiced its American prosperity by establishing in the fifties a small carrying trade between New Bedford and Liberia.

Branded with these evidences of striving for finer living, is an invitation of a difficult character. It is in the fine print which testifies to the fine eyesight of earlier Americans, and announces an Anti-Slavery Anniversary to be held in Music Hall, Boston, January 26, 1859. It is signed by women whose names are among **the immortals:**[13] Helen Eliza Garrison, Maria Weston Chapman, Mary May, L[ydia] Maria Child, and many other women who had invited social ostracism and challenged physical and financial dangers by sponsoring the cause of the Negro.

This matter is of more or less **extraneous**[14] character and belongs, if anywhere, here with the historical collection in the old chest: the early Negro newspapers which were beginning to be published in 1827; the reports of National Conventions of Colored Men held before and soon after the Civil War; copies of the old ballots which elected colored men to the Massachusetts Legislature in the sixties; speeches, state appointments certified by Governor Andrew, Governor Long, Governor Bullock; but, most interesting of all, the old portraits, either daguerreotypes or cards de visite.[15]

How amazingly wide is the range they represent, when one considers the imposed limits and restrictions of Negro life.

Here are portraits of Negro ministers who had spoken not only from leading pulpits in Boston, but in Great Britain, also. Among them is the picture of Boston's first Negro minister, Thomas Paul, in his pulpit in the old

---

[13] **the immortals**—white abolitionists.

[14] **extraneous**—not truly part of.

[15] cards de visite—calling cards, cards with one's name and address given when making visits.

Joy Street Church. Here are portraits of Negro Congressmen, only one of whom was born in Boston, but many of whom had close affiliation with the city, several having sent their children to be educated in the private schools of suburban Boston. These impressive-looking men were leading "Reconstructionists,""Monsters of Corruption," who allowed their ignorant and inexperienced followers to indulge in plush chairs and decorated cuspidors[16] at the expense of the government; men who, for these **laxities**,[17] are still being denounced by a high-minded electorate, but men, nevertheless, who were the first legislators to make laws establishing public schools in their states and laws against land monopolies; men who, according to Louis Post,[18] "forestalled by forty years Lloyd George with his proposal for old-age pensions, and who, by nearly four, preceded Henry George[19] in apprehending the deathly import of land monopoly."

Here are portraits of more Bostonians whose lives were more or less linked with the owners of the old chest: the first Negro graduate of Harvard College, a man of splendid presence, who became one of the terrible **reconstructionists**[20] of South Carolina, and was later sent as a United States Consul to Russia; the first Negro graduate of Harvard Medical School; the first from Harvard Law School, who afterwards became a Massachusetts Judge; the picture of the colored girl who, in 1865, put the features of Colonel Shaw in enduring marble. Here the portrait of a one-time Lieutenant-Governor of a Southern

---

[16] cuspidors—spittoons, containers to spit into.

[17] **laxities**—favors.

[18] Louis Post—scholar who wrote about economics and government at the end of the nineteenth and beginning of the twentieth centuries.

[19] Lloyd George, Henry George—early twentieth-century British politician and nineteenth-century American economist and politician who were involved with economic and welfare reforms.

[20] **reconstructionists**—officials in charge of reestablishing the Southern states as part of the United States following the Civil War.

State, and in the same cover the portrait of another family friend, a Negro who escaped with his wife from slavery and made his way by underground to Boston, where he established his home, an estate which, on the death of the widow, was bequeathed at Harvard College to form a scholarship for Negro boys.

Here, bearded at the age of twenty-three and in the Sergeant's uniform, is the portrait of the family hero who volunteered in '61.

I am stirred and thrilled as this drama of the past unrolls before me: a continuing drama, for herein is a record of a parlor gathering in 1890 of a half dozen Boston colored women, who met to consider some possible way to bring the millions of Negro women into touch with one another for common helpfulness and encouragement—a successful movement begun only thirty years after the Emancipation Proclamation!

Musing in the gathering dusk over these mementos and their associations, my mind by degrees drifts back into the present. It was only the day before that I had been present at one of those modern gatherings where members of the two races meet and, with painful earnestness, struggle, through planned and deliberate efforts, to establish "better race relations." In spite of efforts to approach the subject by new paths and from enlarged points of view, the old "bogey"[21] has reared its head.

"Intermarriage? Socially impossible! The two cultures are not **assimilable**."[22]

And then the ancient **panacea**[23]—"Back to Africa!" Why, after all, is not that the reasonable solution?

Warmed and stirred by these records of men and women who had proved their essential Americanism, I could afford to be amused at the recollection of the

---

[21] bogey—evil spirit.

[22] **assimilable**—mixable, combinable.

[23] **panacea**—remedy, cure-all.

cropping out of these usually irritating "perennials." Much of the failure to "adjust" comes, after all, not only from misunderstanding, but largely from lack of knowledge—lack of knowledge of the diversified phases of Negro life, for one thing. Doubtless my box and its contents may be duplicated in many a home, for all Negro life in America walks hand in hand with tragedy, and all phases are of the deepest significance. And those phases that are richest in suffering and heroism are not always recorded in collections.

It is surprising to find how definite a part of accepted technique has been the closing of eyes and ears and minds to phases of Negro life and character.

Negro life is always picturesque; viewing it, one is conscious of warmth and movement and color. Right here, from the worn contents of this old unconsidered box, there can be obtained a more telling, a more humanly appealing and, possibly, a more socially valuable picture of old Negro Boston, than can be gathered from any number of official records of diligently secured scientific findings.

QUESTIONS TO CONSIDER

1. What kind of story do the contents of the box tell about African Americans in Boston?

2. What do you think is the social class of the family whose history is contained in the box?

3. Why does Ridley believe that her box contains a more valuable picture of old Negro Boston than any "official records of diligently secured scientific findings"?

4. In what way does the physical nature of the box, described in the first paragraph, relate to its contents?

Authors

Frederick Douglass

▲
James Weldon Johnson

W. E. B. DuBois
▼

◀ Langston Hughes

Richard Wright
▼

▲
Frances E. W. Harper

▲
Toni Morrison

▲
Nikki Giovanni

▲
Gwendolyn Brooks

Dorothy West
▼

Rhythms of
Black Life

Second-Hand Man

BY RITA DOVE

Rita Dove (1952–) was the second African American to be awarded the Pulitzer Prize in poetry (1987). She was also distinguished as the first black to be named poet laureate of the United States (1993). A graduate of the University of Iowa Writers' Workshop, Dove writes richly detailed autobiographical and historical poetry. She has also written a collection of short stories and a novel. "Second-Hand Man" is a love story that begins with a young man professing his love for a young lady through performances of music, poetry, and dance.

Virginia couldn't stand it when someone tried to shorten her name—like Ginny, for example. But James didn't. He set his twelve-string guitar down real slow.

"Miss Virginia," he said, "you're a fine piece of woman."

Seemed he'd been asking around. Knew everything about her. Knew she was bold and proud and didn't cotton to no silly negroes. Vir-gin-ee-a he said, nice and slow. Almost Russian, the way he said it. Right then and there she knew this man was for her.

He courted her just inside a year, came by nearly every day. First she wouldn't see him for more than half an hour at a time. She'd send him away; he knew better than to try to force her. Another fellow did that once— kept coming by when she said she had other things to do. She told him he do it once more, she'd be waiting at the door with a pot of **scalding**[1] water to teach him some manners. Did, too. Fool didn't believe her—she had the pot waiting on the stove and when he came up those stairs, she was standing in the door. He took one look at her face and turned and ran. He was lucky those steps were so steep. She only got a little piece of his pant leg.

No, James knew his stuff. He'd come on time and stay till she told him he needed to go.

She'd met him out at Summit Beach one day. In 1921, that was the place to go on hot summer days! Clean yellow sand all around the lake and an amusement park that ran from morning to midnight. She went there with a couple of girl friends. They were younger than her and a little silly. But they were sweet. Virginia was nineteen then. "High time," everyone used to say to her, but she'd just lift her head and go on about her business. She weren't going to marry just any old Negro. He had to be perfect.

There was a man who was chasing her around about that time, too. Tall, dark Negro—Sterling Williams was his name. Pretty as a panther. Married, he was. Least that's what everyone said. Left a wife in Washington, D.C. A little crazy, the wife—poor Sterling was trying to get a divorce.

Well, Sterling was at Summit Beach that day, too. He followed Virginia around, trying to buy her root beer. Everybody loved root beer that summer. Root beer and vanilla ice cream—the Boston Cooler. But she wouldn't

---

[1] **scalding**—very hot; almost boiling.

pay him no mind. People said she was crazy—Sterling was the best catch in Akron, they said.

"Not for me," Virginia said. "I don't want no second-hand man."

But Sterling wouldn't give up. He kept buying root beers and having to drink them himself.

Then she saw James. He'd just come up from Tennessee, working his way up on the riverboats. Folks said his best friend had been lynched down there, and he turned his back on the town and said he was never coming back. Well, when she saw this cute little man in a straw hat and a twelve-string guitar under his arm, she got a little flustered. Her girl friends whispered around to find out who he was, but she acted like she didn't even see him.

He was the hit of Summit Beach. Played that twelve-string guitar like a devil. They'd take off their shoes and sit on the beach toward evening. All the girls loved James. "Oh, Jimmy," they'd squeal, "play us a *loooove* song!" He'd laugh and pick out a tune:

I'll give you a dollar if you'll come out tonight,
If you'll come out tonight,
If you'll come out tonight.
I'll give you a dollar if you'll come out tonight
And dance by the light of the moon.

Then the girls would giggle. "Jimmy," they screamed, "you oughta be 'shamed of yourself!" He'd sing the second verse then:

I danced with a girl with a hole in her stockin',
And her heel kep' a-rockin',
And her heel kep' a-rockin';
I danced with a girl with a hole in her stockin',
And we danced by the light of the moon.

Then they'd all priss and preen[2] their feathers and wonder which would be best—to be in fancy clothes and go on being courted by these dull factory fellows, or to have a hole in their stockings and dance with James.

Virginia never danced. She sat a bit off to one side and watched them make fools of themselves.

Then one night near season's end, they were all sitting down by the water, and everyone had on sweaters and was in a foul mood because the cold weather was coming and there wouldn't be no more parties. Someone said something about hating having the good times end, and James struck up a nice and easy tune, looking across the fire straight at Virginia:

As I was lumb'ring down de street,
Down de street, down de street,
A han'some gal I chanced to meet,
Oh, she was fair to view!

I'd like to make dat gal my wife,
Gal my wife, gal my wife.
I'd be happy all my life
If I had her by me.

She knew he was the man. She'd known it a long while, but she was just biding her time. He called on her the next day. She said she was busy canning peaches. He came back the next day. They sat on the porch and watched the people go by. He didn't say much, except to say her name like that.

"Vir-gin-ee-a," he said, "You're a mighty fine woman."

She sent him home a little after that. He came back a week later. She was angry at him and told him she didn't have time for playing around. But he'd brought his twelve-string guitar, and he said he'd been practicing

---

[2] priss and preen—dress up with great pride, care, and dignity.

all week just to play a couple of songs for her. She let him in then and made him sit on the stool while she sat on the porch swing. He sang the first song. It was a floor thumper.

> There is a gal in our town,
> She wears a yellow striped gown,
> And when she walks the streets aroun',
> The hollow of her foot makes a hole in the
> ground.

> Ol' folks, young folks, cl'ar the kitchen,
> Ol' folks, young folks, cl'ar the kitchen,
> O' Virginny never tire.

She got a little mad then, but she knew he was baiting her. Seeing how much she would take. She knew he wasn't singing about her, and she'd already heard how he said her name. It was time to let the dog in out of the rain, even if he shook his wet all over the floor. So she leaned back and put her hands on her hips, real slow.

"I just *know* you ain't singing about me."

"Virginia," he replied, with a grin would've put Rudolph Valentino[3] to shame, "I'd *never* sing about you that way."

Then he pulled a yellow scarf out his trouser pocket. Like melted butter it was, with fringes.

"I saw it yesterday and thought how nice it would look against your skin," James said.

That was the first present she ever accepted from a man. Then he sang his other song:

> I'm coming, I'm coming!
> Virginia, I'm coming to stay.
> Don't hold it agin' me
> For running away.

---

[3] Rudolph Valentino—handsome movie star of silent pictures known for his role as a romantic lover.

And if I can win ya,
I'll never more roam,
I'm coming Virginia,
My dixie land home.

She was gone for him. Not like those girls on the
beach: she had enough sense left to crack a joke or two.
"You saying I look like the state of Virginia?" she asked,
and he laughed. But she was gone.

She didn't let him know it, though, not for a long
while. Even when he asked her to marry him, eight
months later, he was trembling and thought she just
might refuse out of some woman's whim. No, he courted her proper. Every day for a little while. They'd sit on
the porch until it got too cold, and then they'd sit in the
parlor with two or three bright lamps on. Her mother
and father were glad Virginia'd found a beau, but they
weren't taking any chances. Everything had to be proper.

He got down, all trembly, on one knee and asked her
to be his wife. She said yes. There's a point when all this
dignity and stuff get in the way of Destiny. He kept on
trembling; he didn't believe her.

"What?" James said.

"I said yes," Virginia answered. She was starting to
get angry. Then he saw that she meant it, and he went
into the other room to ask her father for her hand in
marriage.

But people are too curious for their own good, and
there's some things they never need to know, but they're
going to find them out one way or the other. James had
come all the way up from Tennessee and that should
have been far enough, but he couldn't hide that snake
anymore. It just crawled out from under the rock when
it was good and ready.

The snake was Jeremiah Morgan. Some fellows from
Akron had gone off for work on the riverboats, and
some of these fellows had heard about James. That

twelve-string guitar and straw hat of his had made him pretty popular. So, story got to town that James had a baby somewhere. And joined up to this baby—but long dead and buried—was a wife.

Virginia had been married six months when she found out from sweet-talking, side-stepping Jeremiah Morgan who never liked her no-how after she'd laid his soul to rest one night when he'd taken her home from a dance. (She always carried a brick in her purse—no man could get the best of her!)

Jeremiah must have been the happiest man in Akron the day he found out. He found it out later than most people—things like that have a way of circulating first among those who know how to keep it from spreading to the wrong folks—then when the gossip's gotten to everyone else, it's handed over to the one who knows what to do with it.

"Ask that husband of your'n what else he left in Tennessee besides his best friend," was all Jeremiah said at first.

No no-good Negro like Jeremiah Morgan could make Virginia beg for information. She wouldn't bite.

"I ain't got no need for asking my husband nothing," she said, and walked away. She was going to choir practice.

He stood where he was, yelled after her, like any old common person.

"Mrs. Evans always talking about being Number One! It looks like she's Number Two after all."

Her ears burned from the shame of it. She went on to choir practice and sang her prettiest; and straight when she was back home she asked:

"What's all this Number Two business?"

He broke down and told her the whole story—how he'd been married before, when he was seventeen, and his wife dying in childbirth and the child not quite right because of being blue when it was born. And how when his friend was strung up he saw no reason for staying. And how when he met Virginia, he found out pretty quick what she'd done to Sterling Williams and that she'd never have no second-hand man, and he *had* to have her, so he never said a word about his past.

She took off her coat and hung it in the front closet. She unpinned her hat and set it in its box on the shelf. She reached in the back of the closet and brought out his hunting rifle and the box of bullets. She didn't see no way out but to shoot him.

"Put that down!" he shouted. "I love you!"

"You were right not to tell me," she said to him, "because I sure as sin wouldn't have married you. I don't want you *now*."

"Virginia!" he said. He was real scared. "How can you shoot me down like this?"

No, she couldn't shoot him when he stood there looking at her with those sweet brown eyes, telling her how much he loved her.

"You have to sleep sometime," she said, and sat down to wait.

He didn't sleep for three nights. He knew she meant business. She sat up in their best chair with the rifle across her lap, but he wouldn't sleep. He sat at the table and told her over and over that he loved her and he hadn't known what else to do at the time.

"When I get through killing you," she told him, "I'm going to write to Tennessee and have them send that baby up here. It won't do, farming a child out to any relative with an extra plate."

She held onto that rifle. Not that he would have taken it from her—not that that would've saved him. No, the only thing would've saved him was running away. But he wouldn't run either.

Sitting there, Virginia had lots of time to think. He was afraid of what she might do, but he wouldn't leave her, either. Some of what he was saying began to sink in.

He had lied, but that was the only way to get her—she could see the reasoning behind that. And except for that, he was perfect. It was hardly like having a wife before at all. And the baby—anyone could see the marriage wasn't meant to be anyway.

On the third day about midnight, she laid down the rifle.

"You will join the choir and settle down instead of plucking on that guitar anytime anyone drop a hat," she said. "And we will write to your aunt in Tennessee and have that child sent up here." Then she put the rifle back in the closet.

The child never made it up to Ohio—it had died a month before Jeremiah ever opened his mouth. That hit James hard. He thought it was his fault and all, but Virginia made him see the child was sick and was probably better off with its Maker than it would be living out half a life.

James made a good tenor in the choir. The next spring, Virginia had her first baby and they decided to name her Belle. That's French for beautiful. And she was, too.

QUESTIONS TO CONSIDER

1. Why does Virginia select James rather than Sterling as the man she wishes to marry?

2. In what ways is the relationship of James and Virginia a skillful game of flirtation and negotiation?

3. In what ways are Virgina and James both changed after the revelation of James's secret life?

from

The Wedding

BY DOROTHY WEST

*Considered the youngest member of the Harlem Renaissance
Arts Movement of the 1920s, Dorothy West (1909–1998) is
remembered as a skilled novelist, short story writer, and editor.
As a member of Boston's black middle class, West wrote fiction
that critiqued the lives of this growing group of black professionals.
During the early 1930s, West founded* Challenge, an African-American
literary quarterly. *This selection from her novel* The Wedding
*(1995) explores a father's reflections on courtship and marriage
on the eve of his daughter's wedding.*

At the moment Shelby's door closed, Clark Coles placed
his bare foot on the Oak Bluffs beach to begin his morning walk into town. The ferry landing was behind him,
and he could just make out a boat in the distance,
coming with a fresh brace of day trippers from Cape
Cod. Clark hunched his shoulders against a chill wind
blowing in off the water and stooped to roll his left

pants leg up a little farther. He cherished these walks; lately they seemed to be his only chance to get away from the **hubbub**[1] of the wedding. He stopped at a thin white pole that was listing to one side. Pushing it upright with two hands, he swept his foot through the sand to fill in the hole he had created so the pole would stay upright. It was a funny thing, these poles, the way they divided the beach. Corinne would always meet her friends at the twelfth pole, but Shelby and her young group always congregated around the nineteenth, and the young married couples put down their blankets even farther up. Clark guessed that Shelby and Meade would move up themselves next summer—that is, if they came to the island at all.

Clark shook his head. He would never have chosen Meade as a likely mate for his daughter, but it hadn't seemed of late that he'd done a particularly good job choosing a bride himself, so he guessed he couldn't speak as an authority. He glanced at a gnarled piece of driftwood and stepped around it. At least she seemed happy. Was Clark that happy the day before he married Corinne? He honestly couldn't remember. He put his hands in his pockets and rubbed his fingers together. That really wasn't a fair question, he thought, since people today seemed to marry based on a whim, based on some here-today-gone-tomorrow flight of fancy, without a glance at the more practical considerations that seemed to mean everything in Clark's day. The reasons his daughter had for choosing Meade were so different from his and Corinne's that the single word "marriage" seemed insufficient to describe both events, lacking the flexibility to stretch to both poles.

Clark shook his head again. It had all happened so fast. He and several other Northern-educated doctors

---

[1] **hubbub**—noise; confusion.

young enough to be **altruistic**[2] had accepted an invitation to attend a month-long series of panels on modern techniques in medicine at the college where Corinne's father Hannibal was president and Corinne reigned as campus queen.

Clark had been automatically given access to the highest circles of the society in which he found himself. He had all the proper credentials, coming as he did from a family of physicians, all of whom, including his father, were sons of fair Harvard. As the youngest of three brothers, all successful general practitioners who lived **prosperously**[3] on Strivers' Row in Harlem (a street so called because of the prominence and pretensions of this envied and imitated group of professional men and their pretty wives), he was determined to excel in any area that offered a challenge. He was the first of his family to get an office in a white doctors' building downtown, obtained through strings pulled by a fellow grad of Harvard Medical School, and he was on his way to becoming a brilliant **diagnostician**.[4] He was beginning to gain recognition from some of the top men in his field, and he had a growing pool of patients who were willing to ignore his race to **avail**[5] themselves of his talents. Those of his white patients who did not know that he was colored were not too dismayed when they learned it; they decided, as whites generally did, that he was an exception to the general run of his race, a freak, a flash of lightning that would probably not strike his generation again, their knowledge of the colored man and his genes being limited to the creations of their cooks.

---

[2] **altruistic**—unselfish; concerned for others.

[3] **prosperously**—successfully.

[4] **diagnostician**—person who is trained to identify a disease from its signs and symptoms.

[5] **avail**—take advantage of.

Clark's brothers had married attractive, educated women who had given them sons clearly destined for Harvard as well, as evinced by the little crimson emblems[6] sewed on their tiny sweaters. Clark meant to marry better and have at least one more Harvard-bound son than his brothers.

His brothers had all chosen Northern brides, but Clark had a theory, by no means original, that the South produced the colored woman nonpareil.[7] Washington was generally accepted as the place to start the search, the charm and beauty of its women attributed to generous infusions of the blood of senators, men who, though rarely beautiful or charming themselves, managed with the help of their colored mistresses to produce exceptional qualities in their children and their children's children. Yes, the rarefied nature of Washington women was a legend in sophisticated colored circles.

When Clark met Corinne, then, it was a meeting of two perfect people. She was the daughter of a college president, and he could never hope to marry better than that. But neither of them was interested. In Sabina, Corinne's brown classmate, Clark had found the perfect girl-woman, and he wanted to marry her. He had not had time for love before, and until he met Sabina he had never experienced the emotion that is blind to color lines and racial bars and class divisions and religious prejudices and all the other imposed criteria that have nothing to do with love but have so much to do with marriage.

For ten blissful days he saw Sabina whenever their time coincided, and each meeting was a fresh discovery of her sweetness. Her color never crossed his mind except in admiration, and her scholarship status, and the simple background that it implied, made him want to give her more than she had ever had. He knew that

---

[6] crimson emblems—Harvard University symbols.

[7] nonpareil—unequaled; unique.

he had found his girl, and he was almost as sure that he had found his wife. At the unforeseen perfect moment before he returned to New York he intended to propose. He would need all the time he could get in between to pray that she would not refuse.

He could not know that a campaign was planned behind his back to wean this very eligible visitor away from a lowly scholarship student and match him with someone better. And of course there was no one better than Corinne, who was his peer in all the important details, those ironclad facts of background that made the fundamentals of love seem secondary. Every blue-veined hostess[8] was pressed into giving a party for the visiting doctors. In the roundabout **parlance**[9] of politeness, Sabina was not expected at any party. She would not cry foul and claim that she had been deliberately ignored, nor in all fairness could she. She was just one of the many students who did not even know the people who were having the affairs. There wasn't any issue, and to create one would have been unthinkable.

As a visitor from the North, with an imposed obligation to represent the section, the class, the culture from whence he had come, Clark had no gracious way of rejecting the seemingly good intentions of his hosts to display their fabled hospitality. In keeping with the spirit of giving, an animated bouquet of the year's most popular debs[10] was presented to the visiting doctors as dates for the duration. It was inevitable, it was arranged, that Clark would draw Corinne out of the nonexistent hat, for to everyone except themselves their coming together had the full consent of heaven.

Though no one agreed more than Gram, she thought it the better part of wisdom to give heaven human assistance. In June, Corinne would graduate,

---

[8] blue-veined hostess—African-American, upper-class, light-skinned female.

[9] **parlance**—manner of speaking.

[10] debs—debutantes; young women making their formal entrance into society.

and whatever restraints within which Gram held her because of school and study would be in effect no longer. Corinne would come into the ripeness of her twenty-first birthday amid the full-blown summer of the South, which boiled the blood more than the meager summer of the North. Gram was already past seventy, and weary of the night watch. She was quietly resolved to see Corinne married to this mannerly, fair-colored doctor before she had time to make a misstep in the dark of some deep wood with some dark man who would not even try to break her fall. In the long, bedeviling summer of the South, a yielding woman without benefit of miracles could bear the child of many fathers. Gram wanted to see her settled up North, where the ruling passion was ambition and the men sought the smile of success more than the favors of love, finding this **gilded**[11] goddess more fruitful with her golden children than the most abundant woman.

Gram cut her plan of action to the order of Corinne's vanity. She never dwelled on the merits of marriage. Indeed, she had never seen in her own limited relations with Augustus or Josephine's dismal journey into **Nirvana**[12] anything to recommend marriage as a union of loving hearts in which much was given and much was received.

In Corinne's childhood years, the years of dolls and simple pleasures, Gram had never let herself look ahead to the time when Corinne would come into consciousness of herself as a woman, whose logical counterpart was man. Gram had lived without a man in bed beside her, and so had Josephine. Hannibal had always been too buried in someone else's history to care about his own family's future, but Gram cared, and while she knew that Corinne could never marry white, she

---

[11] **gilded**—decorated, adorned.

[12] **Nirvana**—state of detachment.

allowed herself to hope against hope that she'd never marry colored either. But when Corinne reached her riper teens, and boys and clothes and the blossoming of her own beauty became her feverish concern, Gram saw what Hannibal was too preoccupied to see, seeing only Miss Corinne in the aging, worn image of Gram whenever he took the time to look over his glasses. Gram saw that all the dried-out, arrested passion in Hannibal, and in Josephine, and in herself whose life in love had been brief and unrewarding—spent as it was with a man too sorry for himself to give joy to a woman—all that unspent passion had somehow seeped into the blood of this young woman and was now biding in time until it exploded.

Even in Corinne's early teens, when a child, though a child, can still bear a child, Gram had been forced to play the role of watchdog duenna,[13] reluctantly reigning **dowager**[14] in the circle of mothers at parties. She never trusted Corinne to go home with a servant, who could be bribed or cajoled into letting her slip through her fingers. As the better part of wisdom, Gram was forced to encourage Corinne to entertain at home, where she could keep watch in a nearby room, shooing her granddaughter back into a lighted parlor whenever she wandered toward the dark outdoors with a brown boy at the ready (though far from ready for responsibility) breathing hard behind her. That Corinne remained above reproach until the day she married Clark was due in no small part to Gram's unremitting vigilance, and to the obsessive fear it bred of getting caught with a dark boy's baby.

Corinne walked in virtue, but everything in her walk, and in her voice, and in her eyes was a promise of pleasure to come. She seemed the cream of women, a

---

[13] duenna—attendant, chaperone.

[14] **dowager**—an elderly widow of high social station.

woman who had much to give but who would not **squander**[15] it, bred from birth to keep it intact for the man she would marry. She would grace his home with her charm and beauty and she would make his bed joyous, all without ever having to shame his hearth with another man's memory of her shamelessness.

And so she bided her time, waiting for marriage to release her from the cage of her ignorance, to give her the right to make bold inquiry. Then she could free that second self, the dark devourer, the primitive behind the pale skin.

Gram did not know and could not have imagined the size of the monster that stalked Corinne, or the multifold shapes it would assume. All that Gram knew about girls who couldn't wait was what she had seen when a weeping coed was whisked off campus before her rounding belly brought open disgrace to the school. To Gram, the lesson to be learned was that some girls should marry young or come to grief as unwed mothers. Where the embarrassing problem of sex reared its head, the only place to solve it was the marriage bed. Gram's iron will ensured Corinne's restraint, and it also ensured that Clark would not escape from her orbit. Another colored generation would claim a share of Gram's blood, but with her willing it; better to see that blood in the fair-tinted face of a child born with God's blessing than turn to ink in a child turned black as the devil whose thrust had spawned it.

The final end-of-the-season party of the frenetic social whirl that had embraced Clark might have been designed for Gram's purpose. The slightly **hyperthyroid**[16] hostess put all her captive guests through all the ingenious tortures that an all-night party can inflict, winding up the program with scrambled eggs at seven. When Clark brought Corinne home,

---

[15] **squander**—waste.

[16] **hyperthyroid**—extremely active; excited.

obviously tired and clearly showing that she was also tired of Clark, Gram surmised at once that nothing had happened, nothing bad of course, but nothing good either. They had a **lackluster**[17] look to them, nothing like the aura of two people in love. Their feet were too tired from dancing to walk on air, and their heads were too heavy with sleep to care about clouds.

Gram got rid of Corinne by packing her off to Hannibal's study to let him see that his only child had returned to the fold neither maimed nor molested. These extremes had not even occurred to Hannibal, who had slept untroubled throughout the night, unaware that his daughter's virgin bed was empty of its occupant. When she entered his private world he was having breakfast from a tray, a history book propped in front of him. Politely and absently he listened to Corinne, praising her pretty dress; he drew no significance from the hour of its attire. Corinne's voice fell on his ears like the sound of a distant skirmish to a restless sentry,[18] and her image was blurred by the sight of the printed page in front of him.

Alone with Clark, Gram inclined her head toward a chair, and she and Clark sat together in the formal hallway. They both kept their backs ramrod straight, Gram to hold her tired old body together, Clark to keep from falling asleep in the quiet after the long night's clamor. They faced each other across their worlds, the bridge between them lowered for the crossing when Gram permitted Clark to sit in her presence. The significance of her **dispensation**[19] escaped him, though his easy compliance did not escape her. Spearing Clark's eyes with her own, Gram refused to let her mind succumb to weariness until Corinne's future was settled.

---

[17] **lackluster**—dull; unexciting.

[18] restless sentry—soldier on watch who paces back and forth.

[19] **dispensation**—release from the usual obligation (of standing).

Clark braced himself for a dressing down; no doubt this grandam had put two and two together and made the usual error in that kind of nasty, half-cocked addition. It was true enough that some busybodies were trying to make a romance out of his dates with Corinne, forgetting or ignoring the fact that they had been no more to each other than names in a hat. This old lady had probably heard the gossip, which was always two-headed when heard third or fourth hand. And since he had shown no evidence of honorable intentions, made no call on Corinne's father, made no mention of Corinne's meeting his family, he could understand that an anxious grandmother, looking at him in evening clothes in the morning hours, might suspect a wolf underneath the fancy trappings.

She didn't know her granddaughter, he thought to himself. She could handle herself. He hadn't got to first base with her. He hadn't really worked on it, but they were both young and the moon was bright and her lips had barely responded to the kiss he supposed she was expecting when he brought her home from a party. In fact, she seemed to have a thing for dark men. At least she gave them most of her dances. He was lucky if he got her first dance and her last. He didn't mind admitting that he wasn't good at shaking a leg;[20] it made him feel self-conscious, like making love in public. But surely Corinne didn't expect to dance her way through life. Didn't she know that a doctor's hand held as much skill as a dancer's feet? Not that he wanted her to admire him. Not that he wanted her to get serious about him. But he couldn't help but feel **piqued**[21] that he had made so little impression on her. She was pretty enough to be a challenge to any man, and he was male enough to wish he could boast to his friends that he could have had a college president's daughter for the snapping of

---

[20] shaking a leg—dancing.

[21] **piqued**—annoyed; wounded in his pride.

his fingers, except that she was second string to a girl named Sabina.

Sabina . . . He had demanded more than was fair of her understanding. But he had fallen in love with her because there was empathy between them, this communication that silence and separation couldn't alter. She would forgive him this innocent **defection.**[22] He, who had squandered so much of her patience, was impatient to hear her say that he had not. But for Sabina's sake he could not leave until this old woman's unconvinced eyes believed the simple truth that nothing had been created between himself and her granddaughter that could not be ended now and forever. He searched his mind for words that would make clear this total absence of design without being inelegant or ungallant. When they were said and accepted, he would leave their lives with the assumption that he would be forgotten before the falling of the leaves.

"Young man," Gram said, "are you in love with my granddaughter?"

Every thought that Clark had collected flew out of his mind. He felt his face redden like a schoolboy's. "Whatever my feelings," he said wildly, "I'm sure your granddaughter is not in love with me."

"How do you know, young man? Have you asked her?"

"Of course not, ma'am, I wouldn't ask such a conceited question."

"Nonsense! The world wouldn't last very long if everyone were as bashful as you."

That stung him. "I'm not a boy, I'm twenty-eight, ma'am. I'm also a doctor. I could hardly claim to be bashful before women. But I'm also a gentleman. I respect your granddaughter's right to choose for herself without persuasion."

---

[22] **defection**—desertion; abandonment.

"And if she chose you?"

He could think of nothing else to say, so he muttered miserably, "I would be honored."

Gram rose. "I'm very tired, young man. I hope you'll excuse me. I'm old, past seventy. I don't expect to live forever. I want to see my motherless granddaughter settled before I die." She tried to think of his first name: "Carl" or "Clark" or something beginning with C. But it didn't matter, thank God; he too could be called Doctor.

Clark proposed to Corinne after two weeks of escorting her places. In the fourth week a date was set, invitations were sent out, a wedding dress selected, and all the other arrangements of a spectacular happening put in place. The wedding was accomplished without a hitch.

Clark shook himself from his reverie and looked at his watch. He was running late; he had errands to run for Corinne. What was done was done. He was fifty-two. Twenty-four years was long enough for any man to have to live with a mistake. He turned and headed for home, soothed by the thought that if all went as planned his time of penance was almost at an end.

QUESTIONS TO CONSIDER

1. How would you describe color prejudice in the black community based on Clark's observations?

2. Why does Clark make the decision to marry Corinne?

3. What are Clark's remembrances of Sabina years later? Does he have feelings of guilt?

4. In what way are both Sabina and Corinne tragic characters?

Two Poems

BY GWENDOLYN BROOKS

In 1950, poet Gwendolyn Brooks (1917–) became the first African-American woman to receive the Pulitzer Prize. Raised on the south side of Chicago in the "Black Belt" district, Brooks masterfully portrays the struggles and racism encountered by her African-American neighbors and friends. As an artist who chose to stay close to her roots, she supported the Black Power movement of the 1960s. In her later work Brooks explored issues of black consciousness and political empowerment. Her evolving style is seen in "Beverly Hills, Chicago," a traditional poem that highlights the privileges of white life in an affluent Chicago suburb, and "We Real Cool," a free-style verse intended to remind readers of the painful, harsh existence of young, inner-city black men.

Beverly Hills, Chicago

The dry brown coughing beneath their feet,
(Only a while, for the handyman is on his way)
These people walk their golden gardens.
We say ourselves fortunate to be driving by today.

That we may look at them, in their gardens where
The summer ripeness rots. But not raggedly.
Even the leaves fall down in lovelier patterns here.
And the refuse, the refuse is a neat brilliancy.

When they flow sweetly into their houses
With softness and slowness touched by that
    everlasting gold,
We know what they go to. To tea. But that does
    not mean
They will throw some little black dots into some
    water and add sugar and the juice of the cheapest
    lemons that are sold,
While downstairs that woman's vague phonograph
    bleats, "Knock me a kiss."
And the living all to be made again in the sweatingest
    physical manner
Tomorrow. . . . Not that anybody is saying that
    these people have no trouble.
Merely that it is trouble with a gold-flecked
    beautiful banner.

Nobody is saying that these people do not
    ultimately cease to be. And
Sometimes their passings are even more painful
    than ours.
It is just that so often they live till their hair is white.
They make excellent corpses, among the expensive
    flowers. . . .

Nobody is furious. Nobody hates these people.
At least, nobody driving by in this car.
It is only natural, however, that it should occur to us
How much more fortunate they are than we are.

It is only natural that we should look and look
At their wood and brick and stone
And think, while a breath of pine blows,
How different these are from our own.

We do not want them to have less.
But it is only natural that we should think we
    have not enough.
We drive on, we drive on.
When we speak to each other our voices are a
    little gruff.

We Real Cool

We real cool. We
Left school. We

Lurk late. We
Strike straight. We

Sing sin. We
Thin gin. We

Jazz June. We
Die soon.

QUESTIONS TO CONSIDER

1. What are some of the "privileges" of the residents of Beverly Hills, Chicago?

2. How does the narrator convey her feelings of injustice?

3. Why do you think "We Real Cool" consists of a mere twenty-four words? How does it affect the meaning of this poem?

Nikki-Rosa

BY NIKKI GIOVANNI

The quick, intense, pulsating rhythm of Nikki Giovanni's poetry placed her at the center of the black liberation movement of the 1960s. One of the most recognized and popular artists of her generation, Giovanni (1943–) writes and performs her poems, teaches college, and has produced several volumes of children's verse. "Nikki-Rosa" (1968) recognizes a black woman's sense of frustration with the knowledge that white America has the power to "write" and misrepresent her life story.

childhood remembrances are always a drag
if you're Black
you always remember things like living
    in Woodlawn[1]
with no inside toilet
and if you become famous or something
they never talk about how happy you were to have
    your mother all to yourself and

---

[1] Woodlawn—black suburb of Cincinnati.

how good the water felt when you got your
    bath from one of those
big tubs that folk in chicago barbecue in
and somehow when you talk about home
it never gets across how much you
understood their feelings
as the whole family attended meetings about
    Hollydale
and even though you remember
your biographers never understand
your father's pain as he sells his stock
and another dream goes
and though you're poor it isn't poverty that
concerns you
and though they fought a lot
it isn't your father's drinking that makes
    any difference
but only that everybody is together and you
and your sister have happy birthdays and very
    good christmasses
and I really hope no white person ever has
    cause to write about me
because they never understand Black love is
    Black wealth and they'll
probably talk about my hard childhood and
    never understand that all the while I was
    quite happy

QUESTIONS TO CONSIDER

1. What are some of Nikki-Rosa's happy childhood memories?

2. What does Nikki-Rosa want the reader to understand about her childhood?

3. When Nikki-Rosa states, "I really hope no white person ever has cause to write about me," what is her fear?

from

Jazz

BY TONI MORRISON

Author of seven novels and a volume of literary essays, Toni Morrison (1931–   ) became the first African American to win the Nobel Prize in literature in 1993. Her work explores the lives of black people and their communities and celebrates the unique richness of black language and culture. Morrison's storytelling style immediately draws her readers into the major themes that weave themselves throughout her novels, including issues of identity, racism, sexism, spirituality, and African-American folk traditions. As one of the most influential and popular writers of the late twentieth century, Morrison has written novels that give voice to what it means to be black and American. Her sixth novel, Jazz (1992), is about the life of a couple who migrates from the South to New York City during the 1920s Harlem Renaissance.

They met in Vesper County, Virginia, under a walnut tree. She had been working in the fields like everybody else, and stayed past picking time to live with a family twenty miles away from her own. They knew people in common; and suspected they had at least one relative in common. They were drawn together because they had been put together, and all they decided for themselves was when and where to meet at night.

Violet and Joe left Tyrell, a railway stop through Vesper County, in 1906 and boarded the colored section of the Southern Sky. When the train trembled approaching the water surrounding the City, they thought it was like them: nervous at having gotten there at last, but terrified of what was on the other side. Eager, a little scared, they did not even nap during the fourteen hours of a ride smoother than a rocking cradle. The quick darkness in the carriage cars when they shot through a tunnel made them wonder if maybe there was a wall ahead to crash into or a cliff hanging over nothing. The train shivered with them at the thought but went on and sure enough there was ground up ahead and the trembling became the dancing under their feet. Joe stood up, his fingers clutching the baggage rack above his head. He felt the dancing better that way, and told Violet to do the same.

They were hanging there, a young country couple, laughing and tapping back at the tracks, when the attendant came through, pleasant but unsmiling now that he didn't have to smile in this car full of colored people.

"Breakfast in the dining car. Breakfast in the dining car. Good morning. Full breakfast in the dining car." He held a carriage blanket over his arm and from underneath it drew a pint bottle of milk, which he placed in the hands of a young woman with a baby asleep across her knees. "Full breakfast."

He never got his way, this attendant. He wanted the whole coach to file into the dining car, now that they could. Immediately, now that they were out of Delaware and a long way from Maryland there would be no green-as-poison curtain separating the colored people eating from the rest of the diners. The cooks would not feel obliged to pile extra helpings on the plates headed for the curtain; three lemon slices in the iced tea, two pieces of coconut cake arranged to look like one—to take the sting out of the curtain; homey it up with a little extra on the plate. Now, skirting the City, there were no green curtains; the whole car could be full of colored people and everybody on a first-come first-serve basis. If only they would. If only they would tuck those little boxes and baskets underneath the seat; close those paper bags, for once, put the bacon-stuffed biscuits back into the cloth they were wrapped in, and troop single file through the five cars ahead on into the dining car, where the table linen was at least as white as the sheets they dried on juniper bushes; where the napkins were folded with a crease as stiff as the ones they ironed for Sunday dinner; where the gravy was as smooth as their own, and the biscuits did not take second place to the bacon-stuffed ones they wrapped in cloth. Once in a while it happened. Some well-shod woman with two young girls, a preacherly kind of man with a watch chain and a rolled-brim hat might stand up, adjust their clothes and weave through the coaches toward the tables, foamy white with heavy silvery knives and forks. Presided over and waited upon by a black man who did not have to lace his dignity with a smile.

Joe and Violet wouldn't think of it—paying money for a meal they had not missed and that required them to sit still at, or worse, separated by, a table. Not now. Not entering the lip of the City dancing all the way. Her hip bones rubbed his thigh as they stood in the aisle unable to stop smiling. They weren't even there yet and already the City was speaking to them. They were dancing. And like a million others, chests pounding, tracks controlling their feet, they stared out the windows for first sight of the City that danced with them, proving already how much it loved them. Like a million more they could hardly wait to get there and love it back.

Some were slow about it and traveled from Georgia to Illinois, to the City, back to Georgia, out to San Diego and finally, shaking their heads, surrendered themselves to the City. Others knew right away that it was for them, this City and no other. They came on a whim because there it was and why not? They came after much planning, many letters written to and from, to make sure and know how and how much and where. They came for a visit and forgot to go back to tall cotton or short. Discharged with or without honor, fired with or without severance, dispossessed with or without notice, they hung around for a while and then could not imagine themselves anywhere else. Others came because a relative or hometown buddy said, Man, you best see this place before you die; or, We got room now, so pack your suitcase and don't bring no high-top shoes.

However they came, when or why, the minute the leather of their soles hit the pavement—there was no turning around. Even if the room they rented was smaller than the heifer's[1] stall and darker than a morning **privy**,[2] they stayed to look at their number, hear themselves in an audience, feel themselves moving down the street among hundreds of others who moved the way they did, and who, when they spoke, regardless of the accent, treated language like the same intricate, **malleable**[3] toy designed for their play. Part of why they loved it was the specter they left behind. The slumped spines of the veterans of the 27th Battalion[4] betrayed by the commander for whom they had fought like lunatics. The eyes of thousands, stupefied with disgust at having been imported by Mr. Armour, Mr. Swift, Mr. Montgomery Ward[5] to break strikes then dismissed for

---

[1] heifer's—cow's.

[2] **privy**—outhouse.

[3] **malleable**—moldable; flexible.

[4] 27th Battalion—World War I army unit.

[5] Mr. Armour, Mr. Swift, Mr. Montgomery Ward—two prominent Chicago meat packers and a major retailer.

having done so. The broken shoes of two thousand Galveston longshoremen that Mr. Mallory would never pay fifty cents an hour like the white ones. The praying palms, the raspy breathing, the quiet children of the ones who had escaped from Springfield Ohio, Springfield Indiana, Greensburg Indiana, Wilmington Delaware, New Orleans Louisiana, after raving whites had foamed all over the lanes and yards of home.

The wave of black people running from want and violence crested in the 1870s; the '80s; the '90s but was a steady stream in 1906 when Joe and Violet joined it. Like the others, they were country people, but how soon country people forget. When they fall in love with a city, it is for forever, and it is like forever. As though there never was a time when they didn't love it. The minute they arrive at the train station or get off the ferry and glimpse the wide streets and the wasteful lamps lighting them, they know they are born for it. There, in a city, they are not so much new as themselves: their stronger, riskier selves. And in the beginning when they first arrive, and twenty years later when they and the City have grown up, they love that part of themselves so much they forget what loving other people was like—if they ever knew, that is. I don't mean they hate them, no, just that what they start to love is the way a person is in the City; the way a schoolgirl never pauses at a stoplight but looks up and down the street before stepping off the curb; how men accommodate themselves to tall buildings and wee[6] porches, what a woman looks like moving in a crowd, or how shocking her profile is against the backdrop of the East River. The restfulness in kitchen chores when she knows the lamp oil or the staple is just around the corner and not seven miles away; the amazement of throwing open the window and being hypnotized for hours by people on the street below.

[6] wee—small; tiny.

Little of that makes for love, but it does pump desire. The woman who churned a man's blood as she leaned all alone on a fence by a country road might not expect even to catch his eye in the City. But if she is clipping quickly down the big-city street in heels, swinging her purse, or sitting on a stoop with a cool beer in her hand, dangling her shoe from the toes of her foot, the man, reacting to her posture, to soft skin on stone, the weight of the building stressing the delicate, dangling shoe, is captured. And he'd think it was the woman he wanted, and not some combination of curved stone, and a swinging, high-heeled shoe moving in and out of sunlight. He would know right away the **deception**,[7] the trick of shapes and light and movement, but it wouldn't matter at all because the deception was part of it too. . Anyway, he could feel his lungs going in and out. There is no air in the City but there is breath, and every morning it races through him like laughing gas brightening his eyes, his talk, and his expectations. In no time at all he forgets little pebbly creeks and apple trees so old they lay their branches along the ground and you have to reach down or stoop to pick the fruit. He forgets a sun that used to slide up like the yolk of a good country egg, thick and red-orange at the bottom of the sky, and he doesn't miss it, doesn't look up to see what happened to it or to stars made irrelevant by the light of thrilling, wasteful street lamps.

That kind of fascination, permanent and out of control, seizes children, young girls, men of every description, mothers, brides, and barfly women,[8] and if they have their way and get to the City, they feel more like themselves, more like the people they always believed they were. Nothing can pry them away from that; the City is what they want it to be: thriftless, warm, scary and full

---

[7] **deception**—delusion; fantasy.

[8] barfly women—women who spend much time in bars.

of amiable strangers. No wonder they forget pebbly creeks and when they do not forget the sky completely think of it as a tiny piece of information about the time of day or night.

But I have seen the City do an unbelievable sky. Redcaps[9] and dining-car attendants who wouldn't think of moving out of the City sometimes go on at great length about country skies they have seen from the windows of trains. But there is nothing to beat what the City can make of a nightsky. It can empty itself of surface, and more like the ocean than the ocean itself, go deep, starless. Close up on the tops of buildings, near, nearer than the cap you are wearing, such a citysky presses and retreats, presses and retreats, making me think of the free but illegal love of sweethearts before they are discovered. Looking at it, this nightsky booming over a glittering city, it's possible for me to avoid dreaming of what I know is in the ocean, and the bays and tributaries it feeds: the two-seat aeroplanes, nose down in the muck, pilot and passenger staring at schools of passing bluefish; money, soaked and salty in canvas bags, or waving their edges gently from metal bands made to hold them forever. They are down there, along with yellow flowers that eat water beetles and eggs floating away from thrashing fins; along with the children who made a mistake in the parents they chose; along with slabs of Carrara[10] pried from unfashionable buildings. There are bottles too, made of glass beautiful enough to rival stars I cannot see above me because the citysky has hidden them. Otherwise, if it wanted to, it could show me stars cut from the lamé[11] gowns of chorus girls, or mirrored in the eyes of sweethearts **furtive**[12] and happy under the pressure of a deep, touchable sky.

---

[9] Redcaps—baggage porters.

[10] Carrara—white Italian marble.

[11] lamé—shiny metallic fabric.

[12] **furtive**—secret; shifty, sly.

But that's not all a citysky can do. It can go purple and keep an orange heart so the clothes of the people on the streets glow like dance-hall costumes. I have seen women stir shirts into boiled starch or put the tiniest stitches into their hose while a girl straightens the hair of her sister at the stove, and all the while heaven, unnoticed and as beautiful as an Iroquois, drifts past their windows. As well as the windows where sweethearts, free and illegal, tell each other things.

QUESTIONS TO CONSIDER

1. In what ways is this selection similar to jazz music?

2. Why is city life so appealing to Violet and Joe?

3. What does the narrator mean by the statement, "and if they have their way and get to the City, they feel more like themselves, more like the people they always believed they were"?

The Jazz of Poetry

BY JABARI ASIM AND THE LAST POETS

African-American cultural forms share common roots and rhythms.
Jabari Asim links jazz and hip-hop music in his poem "Hip Hop
Bop." Asim weaves contemporary hip-hop language with vibrant
descriptions of clothes (zoot suits, spectator shoes, and porkpie hats)
and nightlife (dances like the lindy-hop and the jitterbug) from
the earlier swing and be-bop era of the 1940s and 1950s. The
Last Poets, Jalal Nuriddin and Suliaman El Hadi, are forefathers
of modern hip-hop music. They are most often recognized for their
socially conscious lyrics. "Jazzoetry" was published in The Last
Poets: Vibes from the Scribes, Selected Poems (1992). This
poem, representative of an oral tradition of African-American
poetry, demonstrates how poetry and jazz music can share the
same structured spontaneity.

Hip Hop Bop

BY JABARI ASIM

well what's up, que pasa[1] & a big hello
habari gani[2] & a hi-dee-ho
share the glory of this story as I break inta rhyme
walkin the new way inside of time
stand back,
or choke on my smoke as I pick up steam
conjurin[3] color, a zoot-suited[4] dream
weavin word spells in a sonic stream
savin the thought nobody caught, puttin it down
beamin a scheme nobody dreamed, givin it sound

I'm a hipster lindy-hoppin[5] in the corner of mind
twirlin toward the exit, strivin ta find
the light of true poetic expression,
breakin the back of systematic oppression
liberatin language, demandin attention
helpin hip hop to another dimension
jazz & rap in combustible conflation[6]
crazyfresh lyrical **prestidigitation**[7]

    Fee Fi Fo Fum
    clap your hands & give the poet some
    poundin percussion like Blakey & Max
        leapin like Lester[8] when he's blowin his axe

---

[1] que pasa—"what's up?" in Spanish.

[2] habari gani—"what's new?" or "what's up?" in the African language Kiswahili.

[3] conjurin—conjuring; calling up or summoning.

[4] zoot-suited—dressed in a man's suit style popular in the 1940s. It was a flashy, extreme style characterized by a long jacket with large, padded shoulders and wide lapels and full trousers that narrowed at the cuffs.

[5] lindy-hoppin—dancing a jitterbug dance that originated in Harlem.

[6] combustible conflation—flammable combination.

[7] **prestidigitation**—trickery.

[8] Blakey & Max . . . Lester—drummers Art Blakey and Max Roach, and jazz saxophonist Lester Young, who were 1950s jazz musicians.

singing like a God, swingin like the devil
juicin this jam to a higher level

rock it don't stop it, rock it don't stop
let me tell you the story of hip hop bop

hip hop boppin's beyond finger poppin
when the rhymes are rockin, there's just no stoppin
the full effect of blues-bombs droppin
& jazz words jumpin like drumsticks pumpin
'scuze me, while I git inta somethin

Jazzoetry

BY THE LAST POETS

Rhythms and sounds
In leaps and bounds
Scales and notes and endless quotes
Hey! Black soul being told

Hypnotising while improvising is mentally
Appetising off on a tangent
Ain't got a cent
Searching, soaring, exploring,
    Seek and you shall find
        More time, more time
            More time, more time
                More time, more time

QUESTIONS TO CONSIDER

1. Why do you think Asim wrote about "breakin the back of systematic oppression" in "Hip Hop Bop"?

2. What concepts or words do these two poems about music share?

3. How are the two poems similar in style?

4. In what way is poetry a better medium than prose for expressing ideas and feelings about jazz (and hip-hop) music?

Looking Back

Moving North A family arrives in Chicago from the rural South around 1920.

◀ This wealthy couple shows the possibilities of financial success in the early twentieth century.

REPRINTED BY PERMISSION OF HOGAN JAZZ ARCHIVE HOWARD-TILTON MEMORIAL LIBRARY TULANE UNIVERSITY.

▲

Throughout the 1920s, many African Americans found housing in
run-down tenements.

◄ King Oliver's Creole Jazz Band was one of the most popular bands of
the 1920s. Its musicians were considered among the best performers to
come out of the Harlem Renaissance.

▲
Farm Work A cotton sharecropper in Georgia cultivates a field with a mule and plow.

A young girl struggles to earn a living by picking cotton in Arkansas. ▶

▲

Farm work After a hard day's work, string bean pickers in Louisiana wait along the highway for their rides home.

◀ A man's hands show the wear and tear of picking cotton.

▲
Housework Some earned a living as domestic servants and caretakers.

◀ A woman in Georgia washes clothes by hand.

City Life An emerging black middle class is growing evidence of financial success and new opportunities.

▲
Church is at the heart of neighborhood life.

◄ Children sit outside a tenement house.

▲
Going to the movies was a popular pastime of many African Americans.
Here a large crowd gathers outside a movie theater in Chicago.

Reflections on Growing Up

from

Notes of a
Native Son

BY JAMES BALDWIN

*James Baldwin (1924–1987) grew up in New York during the
Depression. His love of books and creative writing allowed him
an escape from endless poverty in a strict religious household.
The son of a Pentecostal minister, he was deeply affected by his
father's feelings of anger and powerlessness as a black man
who struggled to support and protect his family. This experience,
along with his intense involvement with the Civil Rights movement
of the 1960s, shaped Baldwin's fiction and political essays. His
harsh critique of social injustices and the plight of black men in
America has given him a place as one of the finest post-World
War II American writers. In "Notes of a Native Son" (1955),
an autobiographical essay, Baldwin confronts his strained
relationship with his father.*

On the 29th of July, in 1943, my father died. On the
same day, a few hours later, his last child was born.
Over a month before this, while all our energies were

concentrated in waiting for these events, there had been, in Detroit, one of the bloodiest race riots of the century. A few hours after my father's funeral, while he lay in state in the undertaker's chapel, a race riot broke out in Harlem. On the morning of the 3rd of August, we drove my father to the graveyard through a wilderness of smashed plate glass. . . .

I had not known my father very well. We had got on badly, partly because we shared, in our different fashions, the vice of stubborn pride. When he was dead I realized that I had hardly ever spoken to him. When he had been dead a long time I began to wish I had. It seems to be typical of life in America, where opportunities, real and fancied, are thicker than anywhere else on the globe, that the second generation has no time to talk to the first. No one, including my father, seems to have known exactly how old he was, but his mother had been born during slavery. He was of the first generation of free men. He, along with thousands of other Negroes, came North after 1919, and I was part of that generation which had never seen the landscape of what Negroes sometimes call the Old Country.

He had been born in New Orleans and had been a quiet young man there during the time that Louis Armstrong,[1] a boy, was running errands for the dives and honky-tonks of what was always presented to me as one of the most wicked of cities—to this day, whenever I think of New Orleans, I also helplessly think of Sodom and Gomorrah.[2] My father never mentioned Louis Armstrong, except to forbid us to play his records; but there was a picture of him on our wall for a long time. One of my father's strong-willed female relatives had placed it there and forbade my father to take it down. He never did, but he eventually maneuvered her

---

[1] Louis Armstrong—famous jazz trumpeter in the 1920s and 1930s.

[2] Sodom and Gomorrah—ancient, wicked cities from Old Testament scripture, Genesis 19: 1–29.

out of the house and when, some years later, she was in trouble and near death, he refused to do anything to help her.

He was, I think, very handsome. I gather this from photographs and from my own memories of him, dressed in his Sunday best and on his way to preach a sermon somewhere, when I was little. Handsome, proud, and ingrown, "like a toe-nail," somebody said. But he looked to me, as I grew older, like pictures I had seen of African tribal chieftains: he really should have been naked, with war-paint on and barbaric mementos, standing among spears. He could be chilling in the pulpit and indescribably cruel in his personal life and he was certainly the most bitter man I have ever met; yet it must be said that there was something else in him, buried in him, which lent him his tremendous power and, even, a rather crushing charm. It had something to do with his blackness, I think—he was very black—with his blackness and his beauty, and with the fact that he knew that he was black but did not know that he was beautiful. He claimed to be proud of his blackness but it had also been the cause of much humiliation and it had fixed bleak boundaries to his life. He was not a young man when we were growing up and he had already suffered many kinds of ruin; in his outrageously demanding and protective way he loved his children, who were black like him and menaced, like him; and all these things sometimes showed in his face when he tried, never to my knowledge with any success, to establish contact with any of us. When he took one of his children on his knee to play, the child always became fretful and began to cry; when he tried to help one of us with our homework the absolutely unabating tension which **emanated**[3] from him caused our minds and our tongues to become paralyzed, so that he, scarcely knowing why, flew into a rage and the child, not knowing why, was

---

[3] **emanated**—came out, flowed out.

punished. If it ever entered his head to bring a surprise home for his children, it was, almost unfailingly, the wrong surprise and even the big watermelons he often brought home on his back in the summertime led to the most appalling scenes. I do not remember, in all those years, that one of his children was ever glad to see him come home. From what I was able to gather of his early life, it seemed that this inability to establish contact with other people had always marked him and had been one of the things which had driven him out of New Orleans. There was something in him, therefore, groping and tentative, which was never expressed and which was buried with him. One saw it most clearly when he was facing new people and hoping to impress them. But he never did, not for long. We went from church to smaller and more improbable church, he found himself in less and less demand as a minister, and by the time he died none of his friends had come to see him for a long time. He had lived and died in an intolerable bitterness of spirit and it frightened me, as we drove him to the graveyard through those unquiet, ruined streets, to see how powerful and overflowing this bitterness could be and to realize that this bitterness now was mine.

When he died I had been away from home for a little over a year. In that year I had had time to become aware of the meaning of all my father's bitter warnings, had discovered the secret of his proudly pursed lips and rigid **carriage:**[4] I had discovered the weight of white people in the world. I saw that this had been for my ancestors and now would be for me an awful thing to live with and that the bitterness which had helped to kill my father could also kill me.

He had been ill a long time—in the mind, as we now realized, reliving instances of his fantastic **intransigence**[5] in the new light of his affliction and

---

[4] **carriage**—manner or behavior; way of carrying oneself.
[5] **intransigence**—extreme, uncompromising position.

endeavoring to feel a sorrow for him which never, quite, came true. We had not known that he was being eaten up by **paranoia**,[6] and the discovery that his cruelty, to our bodies and our minds, had been one of the symptoms of his illness was not, then, enough to enable us to forgive him. The younger children felt, quite simply, relief that he would not be coming home anymore. My mother's observation that it was he, after all, who had kept them alive all these years meant nothing because the problems of keeping children alive are not real for children. The older children felt with my father gone, that they could invite their friends to the house without fear that their friends would be insulted or, as had sometimes happened with me, being told that their friends were in league with the devil and intended to rob our family of everything we owned. (I didn't fail to wonder, and it made me hate him, what on earth we owned that anybody else would want.)

His illness was beyond all hope of healing before anyone realized he was ill. He had always been so strange and had lived, like a prophet in such unimaginably close **communion**[7] with the Lord that his long silences which were punctuated by moans and hallelujahs and snatches of old songs at the living-room window never seemed odd to us. It was not until he refused to eat because, he said, his family was trying to poison him that my mother was forced to accept as a fact what had, until then, been only an unwilling suspicion. When he was committed, it was discovered that he had tuberculosis and, as it turned out, the disease of his mind allowed the rest of his body to destroy him. For the doctors could not force him to eat either, and, though he was fed intravenously, it was clear from the beginning that there was no hope for him.

---

[6] **paranoia**—mental illness characterized by feelings of persecution.

[7] **communion**—fellowship; attachment.

In my mind's eye I could see him, sitting at the window, locked up in his terrors; hating and fearing every living soul including his children who had betrayed him, too, by reaching toward the world which had despised him. There were nine of us. I began to wonder what it could have felt like for a man to have had nine children whom he could barely feed. He used to make little jokes about our poverty, which never, of course, seemed very funny to us; they could not have seemed very funny to him, either, or else our all too feeble response to them would never have caused such rages. He spent great energy and achieved, to our **chagrin**,[8] no small amount of success in keeping us away from the people who surrounded us, people who had all-night rent parties[9] to which we listened when we should have been sleeping, people who cursed and drank and flashed razor blades on Lenox Avenue. He could not understand why, if they had so much energy to spare, they could not use it to make their lives better. He treated almost everybody on our block with a most uncharitable **asperity**[10] and neither they, nor, of course, their children were slow to reciprocate.

The only white people who came to our house were welfare workers and bill collectors. It was almost always my mother who dealt with them, for my father's temper, which was at the mercy of his pride, was never to be trusted. It was clear that he felt their very presence in his home to be a violation: this was conveyed by his carriage, almost ludicrously stiff, and by his voice, harsh and vindictively polite. When I was around nine or ten I wrote a play which was directed by a young, white schoolteacher, a woman, who then took an interest in me, and gave me books to read and, in order to

---

[8] **chagrin**—embarrassment and disappointment.

[9] rent parties—parties given by people to raise money to pay the rent. The guests would pay a fee to enjoy the food and entertainment.

[10] **asperity**—bitterness; ill temper.

corroborate[11] my theatrical bent, decided to take me to see what she somewhat tactlessly referred to as "real" plays. Theater-going was forbidden in our house, but, with the really cruel intuitiveness of a child, I suspected that the color of this woman's skin would carry the day for me. When, at school, she suggested taking me to the theater, I did not, as I might have done if she had been a Negro, find a way of discouraging her, but agreed that she should pick me up at my house one evening. I then, very cleverly, left all the rest to my mother, who suggested to my father, as I knew she would, that it would not be very nice to let such a kind woman make the trip for nothing. Also, since it was a school teacher, I imagined that my mother countered the idea of sin with the idea of "education," which word, even with my father, carried a kind of bitter weight.

Before the teacher came my father took me aside to ask *why* she was coming, what *interest* she could possibly have in our house, in a boy like me. I said I didn't know but I, too, suggested that it had something to do with education. And I understood that my father was waiting for me to say something—I didn't quite know what; perhaps that I wanted his protection against this teacher and her "education." I said none of these things and the teacher came and we went out. It was clear, during the brief interview in our living room, that my father was agreeing very much against his will and that he would have refused permission if he had dared. The fact that he did not dare caused me to despise him: I had no way of knowing that he was facing in that living room a wholly unprecedented and frightening situation.

"But as for me and my house," my father had said, "we will serve the Lord."[12] I wondered, as we drove him to his resting place, what this line had meant for him. I

---

[11] **corroborate**—establish; strengthen.

[12] "But as for me and my house . . . we will serve the Lord."—Old Testament scripture, Joshua 24:15.

had heard him preach it many times. I had preached it once myself, proudly giving it an interpretation different from my father's. Now the whole thing came back to me, as though my father and I were on our way to Sunday school and I were memorizing the golden text: *And if it seem evil unto you to serve the Lord, choose you this day whom you will serve; whether the gods which your fathers served that were on the other side of the flood, or the gods of the Amorites, in whose land ye dwell: but as for me and my house, we will serve the Lord.* I suspected in these familiar lines a meaning which had never been there for me before. All of my father's texts and songs, which I had decided were meaningless, were arranged before me at his death like empty bottles, waiting to hold the meaning which life would give them for me. This was his legacy: nothing is ever escaped. That bleakly memorable morning I hated the unbelievable streets and the Negroes and whites who had, equally, made them that way. But I knew that it was folly, as my father would have said, this bitterness was folly. It was necessary to hold on to the things that mattered. The dead man mattered, the new life mattered; blackness and whiteness did not matter; to believe that they did was to **acquiesce**[13] in one's own destruction. Hatred, which could destroy so much, never failed to destroy the man who hated and this was an **immutable**[14] law.

It began to seem that one would have to hold in the mind forever two ideas which seemed to be in opposition. The first idea was acceptance, the acceptance, totally without **rancor**,[15] of life as it is, and men as they are: in the light of this idea, it goes without saying that injustice is a commonplace. But this did not mean that one could be **complacent**,[16] for the second idea was of equal

---

[13] **acquiesce**—consent.

[14] **immutable**—unchangeable.

[15] **rancor**—resentment.

[16] **complacent**—self-satisfied, unconcerned.

power: that one must never, in one's own life, accept these injustices as commonplace but must fight them with all one's strength. This fight begins, however, in the heart and it now had been laid to my charge to keep my own heart free of hatred and despair. This **intimation**[17] made my heart heavy and, now that my father was irrecoverable, I wished that he had been beside me so that I could have searched his face for the answers which only the future would give me now.

---

[17] **intimation**—subtle, indirect suggestion.

QUESTIONS TO CONSIDER

1. What positive memories does James Baldwin have of his father?

2. What was the tragedy of his father's life?

3. Why do you think it was important for Baldwin to come to terms with his father's life?

Why I Like Country Music

BY JAMES ALAN McPHERSON

Although James McPherson (1943–   ) received a law degree from Harvard in the late sixties, he made the decision to devote his career to writing and teaching fiction. An acclaimed short story writer, McPherson received the Pulitzer Prize for his second collection of stories, entitled Elbow Room. *"Why I Like Country Music" (1977), from this collection, is a coming-of-age story about a boy growing up in the South.*

My dear, dear Gloria, her name was Gweneth Lawson:

She was a pretty, chocolate brown little girl with dark brown eyes and two long black braids. After all these years, the image of these two braids **evokes**[1] in me all there is to remember about Gweneth Lawson. They were plaited across the top of her head and hung to a

---

[1] **evokes**—provokes; calls out.

point just above the back of her Peter Pan collar. Sometimes she wore two bows, one red and one blue, and these tended to sway lazily near the place on her neck where the smooth brown of her skin and the white of her collar met the ink-bottle black of her hair. Even when I cannot remember her face, I remember the rainbow of deep, rich colors in which she lived. This is so because I watched them, every weekday, from my desk directly behind hers in our fourth-grade class. And she wore the most magical perfume, or lotion, smelling just slightly of fresh-cut lemons, that wafted back to me whenever she made the slightest movement at her desk. Now I must tell you this much more, dear Gloria: whenever I smell fresh lemons, whether in the market or at home, I look around me—not for Gweneth Lawson, but for some quiet corner where I can revive in private certain memories of her. And in pursuing these memories across such lemony bridges, I rediscover that I loved her.

Gweneth was from the South Carolina section of Brooklyn.[2] Her parents had sent her south to live with her uncle, Mr. Richard Lawson, the brick mason, for an unspecified period of time. Just why they did this I do not know, unless it was their plan to have her absorb more of South Carolina folkways than conditions in Brooklyn would allow. She was a gentle, soft-spoken girl; I recall no **condescension**[3] in her manner. This was all the more admirable because our unrestrained awe of a Northern-born black person usually induced in him some grand sense of his own importance. You must know that in those days older folks would point to someone and say, "He's from the North," and the statement would be sufficient in itself. Mothers made their children behave by advising that, if they led exemplary lives and attended church regularly, when they died

---

[2] Brooklyn—a borough in New York City.

[3] **condescension**—conceit, arrogance.

they would go to New York. Only someone who understands what London meant to Dick Whittington,[4] or how California and the suburbs function in the national mind, could appreciate the mythical dimensions of this Northlore.

But Gweneth Lawson was above regional idealization. Though I might have loved her partly because she was a Northerner, I loved her more because of the world of colors that seemed to be suspended about her head. I loved her glowing forehead and I loved her bright, dark brown eyes; I loved the black braids, the red and blue and sometimes yellow and pink ribbons; I loved the way the deep, rich brown of her neck melted into the pink or white cloth of her Peter Pan collar; I loved the lemony vapor on which she floated and from which on occasion, she seemed to be inviting me to be buoyed up, up, up into her happy world; I loved the way she caused my heart to tumble whenever, during a restless moment, she seemed about to turn her head in my direction; I loved her more, though torturously, on the many occasions when she did not turn. Because I was a shy boy, I loved the way I could love her silently, at least six hours a day, without ever having to disclose my love.

My **platonic**[5] state of mind might have stretched onward into a blissful infinity had not Mrs. Esther Clay Boswell, our teacher, made it her business to pry into the affair. Although she prided herself on being a strict disciplinarian, Mrs. Boswell was not without a sense of humor. A round, full-breasted woman in her early forties, she liked to amuse herself, and sometimes the class as well, by calling the attention of all eyes to whomever of us violated the structure she imposed on classroom activities. She was particularly hard on people like me who could not contain an impulse to daydream, or

---

[4] Dick Whittington—former London mayor (1397) who, according to legend, came to London after hearing the streets were paved with gold.

[5] **platonic**—purely spiritual thoughts or desires.

those who allowed their eyes to wander too far away from lessons printed on the blackboard. A black and white sign posted under the electric clock next to the door summed up her attitude toward this kind of truancy: NOTICE TO ALL CLOCKWATCHERS, it read, TIME PASSES, WILL YOU? Nor did she **abide**[6] timidity in her students. Her voice booming, "Speak up, boy!" was more than enough to cause the more emotional among us, including me, to break into convenient flows of warm tears. But by doing this we violated yet another rule, one on which depended our very survival in Mrs. Esther Clay Boswell's class. She would spell out this rule for us as she paced before her desk, slapping a thick, homemade ruler against the flat of her brown palm. "There ain't no *babies* in here," she would recite. *Thaap!* "Anybody thinks he's still a *baby* . . ." *Thaap!* ". . . should crawl back home to his mama's [breast]." *Thaap!* "You little bunnies shed your *last water* . . ."[7] *Thaap!* ". . . the minute you left home to come in here." *Thaap!* "From now on, you g'on do all your *cryin'* . . ." *Thaap!* ". . . in *church!*" *Thaap!* Whenever one of us compelled her to make this speech it would seem to me that her eyes paused overlong on my face. She would seem to be daring me, as if suspicious that, in addition to my secret passion for Gweneth Lawson, which she might excuse, I was also in the habit of throwing fits of temper.

She had read me right. I was the product of too much attention from my father. He favored me, paraded me around on his shoulder, inflated my ego constantly with what, among us at least, was a high compliment: "You my [boy] if you don't get no bigger." This statement, along with my father's generous attentions, made me selfish and used to having my own way. I *expected* to have my own way in most things, and when I could not,

---

[6] **abide**—tolerate.

[7] last water—tears.

I tended to throw tantrums calculated to break through any barrier raised against me.

Mrs. Boswell was also perceptive in assessing the extent of my infatuation with Gweneth Lawson. Despite my **stealth**[8] in telegraphing emissions of affection into the back part of Gweneth's brain, I could not help but observe, occasionally, Mrs. Boswell's cool glance pausing on the two of us. But she never said a word. Instead, she would settle her eyes momentarily on Gweneth's face and then pass quickly to mine. But in that instant she seemed to be saying, "Don't look back now, girl, but I *know* that bald-headed boy behind you has you on his mind." She seemed to watch me daily, with a combination of amusement and absolute detachment in her brown eyes. And when she stared, it was not at me but at the normal focus of my attention: the end of Gweneth Lawson's black braids. Whenever I sensed Mrs. Boswell watching I would look away quickly, either down at my brown desk top or across the room to the blackboard. But her eyes could not be eluded this easily. Without looking at anyone in particular, she could make a specific point to one person in a manner so general that only long afterward did the real object of her attention realize it had been intended for him.

"Now you little brown bunnies," she might say, "and you black buck rabbits and you few cottontails mixed in, some of you starting to smell yourselves under the arms without knowing what it's all about." And here, it sometimes seemed to me, she allowed her eyes to pause casually on me before resuming their sweep of the entire room. "Now I know your mamas already made you think life is a bed of roses, but in *my* classroom you got to know the foot-paths through the *sticky* parts of the rose-bed." It was her custom during this ritual to prod and goad those of us who were

---

[8] **stealth**—secrecy, slyness.

developing reputations for meekness and indecision; yet her method was Socratic[9] in that she compelled us, indirectly, to supply our own answers by exploiting one person as the walking symbol of the error she intended to correct. Clarence Buford, for example, an oversized but good-natured boy from a very poor family, served often as the helpmeet in this exercise.

"Buford," she might begin, slapping the ruler against her palm, "how does a tongue-tied country boy like you expect to get a wife?"

"I don't want no wife," Buford might grumble softly. Of course the class would laugh.

"Oh yes you do," Mrs. Boswell would respond. "All you buck rabbits want wives. " *Thaap*! "So how do you let a girl know you not just a bump on a log?"

"I know! I know!" a high voice might call from a seat across from mine. This, of course, would be Leon Pugh. A peanut-brown boy with curly hair, he seemed to know everything. Moreover, he seemed to take pride in being the only one who knew answers to life questions and would wave his arms excitedly whenever our attentions were focused on such matters. It seemed to me his voice would be extra loud and his arms waved more strenuously whenever he was certain that Gweneth Lawson, seated across from him, was interested in an answer to Mrs. Esther Clay Boswell's question. His eager arms, it seemed to me, would be reaching out to grasp Gweneth instead of the question asked.

"Buford, you twisted-tongue, bunion-toed country boy," Mrs. Boswell might say, ignoring Leon Pugh's hysterical armwaving, "you gonna let a cottontail like Leon get a girlfriend before you?"

"I don't want no girlfriend," Clarence Buford would almost sob. "I don't like no girls."

---

[9] Socratic—like that of the ancient Greek philosopher and teacher Socrates. The Socratic method uses questions and answers to guide students toward the things they must learn.

The class would laugh again while Leon Pugh manipulated his arms like a flight navigator under battle conditions. "I know! I know! I swear to *God* I know!"

When at last Mrs. Boswell would turn in his direction, I might sense that she was tempted momentarily to ask me for an answer. But as in most such exercises, it was the worldly-wise Leon Pugh who supplied this. "What do *you* think, Leon?" she would ask inevitably, but with a rather lifeless slap of the ruler against her palm.

"My daddy told me . . ." Leon would shout, turning slyly to beam at Gweneth, ". . . my daddy and my big brother from the Bronx New York told me that to git *anythin'* in this world you gotta learn how to blow your own horn."

"Why, Leon?" Mrs. Boswell might ask in a bored voice.

"Because," the little boy would recite, puffing out his chest, "because if you don't blow your own horn ain't nobody else g'on blow it for you. That's what my daddy said."

"What do you think about that, Buford?" Mrs. Boswell would ask.

"I don't want no girlfriend anyhow," the puzzled Clarence Buford might say.

And then the **cryptic**[10] lesson would suddenly be dropped.

This was Mrs. Esther Clay Boswell's method of teaching. More than anything written on the blackboard, her questions were calculated to make us turn around in our chairs and inquire in guarded whispers of each other, and especially of the wise and confident Leon Pugh, "What does she mean?" But none of us, besides Pugh, seemed able to comprehend what it was we ought to know but did not know. And Mrs. Boswell, plump brown fox that she was, never volunteered any

---

[10] **cryptic**—puzzling, unclear.

more in the way of confirmation than was necessary to keep us interested. Instead, she paraded around us, methodically slapping the homemade ruler against her palm, suggesting by her silence more depth to her question, indeed, more implications in Leon's answer, than we were then able to perceive. And during such moments, whether inspired by selfishness or by the peculiar way Mrs. Boswell looked at me, I felt that finding answers to such questions was a task she had set for me, of all the members of the class.

Of course Leon Pugh, among other lesser lights, was my chief rival for the affections of Gweneth Lawson. All during the school year, from September through the winter rains, he bested me in my attempts to look directly into her eyes and say a simple, heartfelt, "hey." This was my ambition, but I never seemed able to get close enough to her attention. At Thanksgiving I helped draw a bounteous yellow **cornucopia**[11] on the blackboard, with fruits and flowers matching the colors that floated around Gweneth's head; Leon Pugh made one by himself, a masterwork of silver paper and multicolored crepe, which he hung on the door. Its silver tail curled upward to a point just below the face of Mrs. Boswell's clock. At Christmas, when we drew names out of a hat for the exchange of gifts, I drew the name of Queen Rose Phipps, a fairly unattractive squash-yellow girl of absolutely no interest to me. Pugh, whether through **collusion**[12] with the boy who handled the lottery or through pure luck, pulled forth from the hat the magic name of Gweneth Lawson. He gave her a set of deep purple bows for her braids and a basket of pecans from his father's tree. Uninterested now in the spirit of the occasion, I delivered to Queen Rose Phipps a pair of white socks. Each

---

[11] **cornucopia**—horn-shaped basket overflowing with fruit and flowers.

[12] **collusion**—secret agreement for deceitful or illegal purpose.

time Gweneth wore the purple bows she would glance over at Leon and smile. Each time Queen Rose wore my white socks I would turn away in embarrassment, lest I should see them pulling down into her shoes and exposing her skinny ankles.

After class, on wet winter days, I would trail along behind Gweneth to the bus stop, pause near the steps while she entered, and follow her down the aisle until she chose a seat. Usually, however, in clear violation of the code of conduct to which all gentlemen were expected to adhere, Leon Pugh would already be on the bus and shouting to passersby, "Move off! Get away! This here seat by me is reserved for the girl from Brooklyn New York." Discouraged but not defeated, I would swing into the seat next nearest her and cast calf-eyed glances of wounded affection at the back of her head or at the brown, rainbow profile of her face. And at her stop, some eight or nine blocks from mine, I would disembark behind her along with a crowd of other love-struck boys. There would then follow a well-rehearsed scene in which all of us save Leon Pugh, pretended to have gotten off the bus either too late or too soon to wend our proper paths homeward. And at slight cost to ourselves we enjoyed the advantage of being able to walk close by her as she glided toward her uncle's green-frame house. There, after pausing on the wooden steps and smiling radiantly around the crowd like a spring sun in that cold winter rain, she would sing, "Bye, y'all," and disappear into the structure with the mystery of a goddess. Afterward I would walk away, but slowly, much slower than the other boys, warmed by the music and light in her voice against the sharp wet winds of the February afternoon.

I loved her, dear Gloria, and I danced with her and smelled the lemony youth of her and told her that I loved her, all this in a way you would never believe.

QUESTIONS TO CONSIDER

1. What is the importance of Mrs. Esther Clay Boswell's relationship with the narrator?

2. Why are the narrator's remembrances of Gweneth Lawson still magical after so many years?

3. How is Leon Pugh different from the other boys in his class?

Beauty: When the Other Dancer Is the Self

BY ALICE WALKER

As the daughter of a tenant farmer and domestic worker from rural Georgia, Alice Walker (1944–   ) witnessed the women in her community turn to gardening and quilting as a way of expressing their creative powers in a society that recognized them only as laborers. Walker's fiction, essays, short stories and poetry are a response to the condition of black women's lives. In 1983 Walker received the Pulitzer Prize for her novel The Color Purple. *She also received acclaim for resurrecting the work of Zora Neale Hurston, one of the most important novelists and folklorists of the Harlem Renaissance. Walker's autobiographical essay on beauty (1983) is a remembrance of a painful childhood accident.*

It is a bright summer day in 1947. My father, a fat, funny man with beautiful eyes and a **subversive**[1] wit, is trying to decide which of his eight children he will take

---

[1] **subversive**—rebellious, defiant.

with him to the county fair. My mother, of course, will not go. She is knocked out from getting most of us ready: I hold my neck stiff against the pressure of her knuckles as she hastily completes the braiding and then beribboning of my hair.

My father is the driver for the rich old white lady up the road. Her name is Miss Mey. She owns all the land for miles around, as well as the house in which we live. All I remember about her is that she once offered to pay my mother thirty-five cents for cleaning her house, raking up piles of her magnolia leaves, and washing her family's clothes, and that my mother—she of no money, eight children, and a chronic earache—refused it. But I do not think of this in 1947. I am two and a half years old. I want to go everywhere my daddy goes. I am excited at the prospect of riding in a car. Someone has told me fairs are fun. That there is room in the car for only three of us doesn't faze me at all. Whirling happily in my starchy frock, showing off my biscuit-polished patent-leather shoes and lavender socks, tossing my head in a way that makes my ribbons bounce, I stand, hands on hips, before my father. "Take me, Daddy," I say with assurance; "I'm the prettiest!"

Later, it does not surprise me to find myself in Miss Mey's shiny black car, sharing the back seat with the other lucky ones. Does not surprise me that I thoroughly enjoy the fair. At home that night I tell the unlucky ones all I can remember about the merry-go-round, the man who eats live chickens, and the teddy bears, until they say: that's enough, baby Alice. Shut up now, and go to sleep.

It is Easter Sunday, 1950. I am dressed in a green, flocked scalloped-hem dress (handmade by my adoring sister, Ruth) that has its own smooth satin petticoat and tiny hot-pink roses tucked into each scallop. My shoes, new T-strap patent leather, again highly biscuit-polished. I am six years old and have learned one of the longest Easter speeches to be heard that day, totally unlike the speech I said when I was two: "Easter lilies/pure and white/blossom in/the morning light." When I rise to give my speech I do so on a great wave of love and pride and expectation. People in the church stop rustling their new crinolines.[2] They seem to hold their breath. I can tell they admire my dress, but it is my spirit, bordering on sassiness (womanishness), they secretly applaud.

"That girl's a little *mess*," they whisper to each other, pleased.

Naturally I say my speech without stammer or pause, unlike those who stutter, stammer, or, worst of all, forget. This is before the word "beautiful" exists in people's vocabulary, but "Oh, isn't she the *cutest* thing!" frequently floats my way. "And got so much sense!" they gratefully add . . . for which thoughtful addition I thank them to this day.

It was great fun being cute. But then, one day, it ended.

I am eight years old and a tomboy. I have a cowboy hat, cowboy boots, checkered shirt and pants, all red. My playmates are my brothers, two and four years older than I. Their colors are black and green, the only difference in the way we are dressed. On Saturday nights we all go to the picture show, even my mother; Westerns are her favorite kind of movie. Back home, "on the ranch," we pretend we are Tom Mix, Hopalong Cassidy, Lash LaRue[3] (we've even named one of our dogs Lash LaRue); we chase each other for hours rustling cattle, being outlaws, delivering damsels[4] from distress. Then my parents decide to buy my brothers guns. These are not "real" guns. They shoot "BBs," copper pellets my brothers say will kill birds. Because I am a girl, I do not

---

[2] crinolines—full, stiff underskirts or slips worn under a skirt or dress.

[3] Tom Mix, Hopalong Cassidy, Lash LaRue—famous western movie heroes of the 1950s.

[4] damsels—young women.

get a gun. Instantly I am **relegated**[5] to the position of Indian. Now there appears a great distance between us. They shoot and shoot at everything with their new guns. I try to keep up with my bow and arrows.

One day while I am standing on top of our makeshift "garage"—pieces of tin nailed across some poles—holding my bow and arrow and looking out toward the fields, I feel an incredible blow in my right eye. I look down just in time to see my brother lower his gun.

Both brothers rush to my side. My eye stings, and I cover it with my hand. "If you tell," they say, "we will get a whipping. You don't want that to happen, do you?" I do not. "Here is a piece of wire," says the older brother, picking it up from the roof; "say you stepped on one end of it and the other flew up and hit you." The pain is beginning to start. "Yes," I say. "Yes, I will say that is what happened." If I do not say this is what happened, I know my brothers will find ways to make me wish I had. But now I will say anything that gets me to my mother.

Confronted by our parents we stick to the lie agreed upon. They place me on a bench on the porch and I close my left eye while they examine the right. There is a tree growing from underneath the porch that climbs past the railing to the roof. It is the last thing my right eye sees. I watch as its trunk, its branches, and then its leaves are blotted out by the rising blood.

I am in shock. First there is intense fever, which my father tries to break using lily leaves bound around my head. Then there are chills: my mother tries to get me to eat soup. Eventually, I do not know how, my parents learn what has happened. A week after the "accident" they take me to see a doctor. "Why did you wait so long to come?" he asks, looking into my eye and shaking his

---

[5] **relegated**—assigned; made to be.

head. "Eyes are sympathetic," he says. "If one is blind, the other will likely become blind too."

This comment of the doctor's terrifies me. But it is really how I look that bothers me most. Where the BB pellet struck there is a glob of whitish scar tissue, a hideous cataract,[6] on my eye. Now when I stare at people—a favorite pastime, up to now—they will stare back. Not at the "cute" little girl, but at her scar. For six years I do not stare at anyone, because I do not raise my head.

Years later, in the throes of a mid-life crisis, I ask my mother and sister whether I changed after the "accident." "No," they say, puzzled. "What do you mean?"

What do I mean?

I am eight, and, for the first time, doing poorly in school, where I have been something of a whiz since I was four. We have just moved to the place where the "accident" occurred. We do not know any of the people around us because this is a different county. The only time I see the friends I knew is when we go back to our old church. The new school is the former state **penitentiary.**[7] It is a large stone building, cold and drafty, crammed to overflowing with **boisterous,**[8] ill-disciplined children. On the third floor there is a huge circular imprint of some partition that has been torn out.

"What used to be here?" I ask a sullen girl next to me on our way past it to lunch.

"The electric chair," says she.

At night I have nightmares about the electric chair, and about all the people reputedly "fried" in it. I am afraid of the school, where all the students seem to be budding criminals.

---

[6] cataract—cloudy condition in the lens of the eye causing visual impairment.

[7] **penitentiary**—prison.

[8] **boisterous**—loud, noisy.

"What's the matter with your eye?" they ask, critically.

When I don't answer (I cannot decide whether it was an "accident" or not), they shove me, insist on a fight.

My brother, the one who created the story about the wire, comes to my rescue. But then brags so much about "protecting" me, I become sick.

After months of torture at the school, my parents decide to send me back to our old community, to my old school. I live with my grandparents and the teacher they board. But there is no room for Phoebe, my cat. By the time my grandparents decide there *is* room and I ask for my cat, she cannot be found. Miss Yarborough, the boarding teacher, takes me under her wing, and begins to teach me to play the piano. But soon she marries an African—a "prince," she says—and is whisked away to his continent.

At my old school there is at least one teacher who loves me. She is the teacher who "knew me before I was born" and bought my first baby clothes. It is she who makes life bearable. It is her presence that finally helps me turn on the one child at the school who continually calls me "one-eyed [expletive]." One day I simply grab him by his coat and beat him until I am satisfied. It is my teacher who tells me my mother is ill.

My mother is lying in bed in the middle of the day, something I have never seen. She is in too much pain to speak. She has an abscess[9] in her ear. I stand looking down on her, knowing that if she dies, I cannot live. She is being treated with warm oils and hot bricks held against her cheek. Finally a doctor comes. But I must go back to my grandparents' house. The weeks pass but I am hardly aware of it. All I know is that my mother might die, my father is not so jolly, my brothers still have their guns, and I am the one sent away from home.

---

[9] abscess—infection.

"You did not change," they say.

Did I imagine the anguish of never looking up?

I am twelve. When relatives come to visit I hide in my room. My cousin Brenda, just my age, whose father works in the post office and whose mother is a nurse, comes to find me. "Hello," she says. And then she asks, looking at my recent school picture, which I did not want taken, and on which the "glob," as I think of it, is clearly visible, "You still can't see out of that eye?"

"No," I say, and flop back on the bed over my book.

That night, as I do almost every night, I abuse my eye. I rant and rave at it, in front of the mirror. I plead with it to clear up before morning. I tell it I hate and despise it. I do not pray for sight. I pray for beauty.

"You did not change," they say.

I am fourteen and baby-sitting for my brother Bill, who lives in Boston. He is my favorite brother and there is a strong bond between us. Understanding my feelings of shame and ugliness he and his wife take me to a local hospital, where the "glob" is removed by a doctor named O. Henry. There is still a small bluish crater where the scar tissue was, but the ugly white stuff is gone. Almost immediately I become a different person from the girl who does not raise her head. Or so I think. Now that I've raised my head I win the boyfriend of my dreams. Now that I've raised my head I have plenty of friends. Now that I've raised my head classwork comes from my lips as faultlessly as Easter speeches did, and I leave high school as valedictorian, most popular student, and *queen*, hardly believing my luck. Ironically, the girl who was voted most beautiful in our class (and was) was later shot twice through the chest by a male companion, using a "real" gun, while she was pregnant. But that's another story in itself. Or is it?

"You did not change," they say.

It is now thirty years since the "accident." A beautiful journalist comes to visit and to interview me. She is going to write a cover story for her magazine that focuses on my latest book. "Decide how you want to look on the cover," she says. "Glamorous, or whatever."

Never mind "glamorous," it is the "whatever" that I hear. Suddenly all I can think of is whether I will get enough sleep the night before the photography session: if I don't, my eye will be tired and wander, as blind eyes will.

At night in bed with my lover I think up reasons why I should not appear on the cover of a magazine. "My meanest critics say I've sold out," I say. "My family will now realize I write scandalous books."

"But what's the real reason you don't want to do this?" he asks.

"Because in all probability," I say in a rush, "my eye won't be straight."

"It will be straight enough," he says. Then, "Besides, I thought you'd made your peace with that."

And I suddenly remember that I have.

I remember:

I am talking to my brother Jimmy, asking if he remembers anything unusual about the day I was shot. He does not know I consider that day the last time my father, with his sweet home remedy of cool lily leaves, chose me, and that I suffered and raged inside because of this. "Well," he says, "all I remember is standing by the side of the highway with Daddy, trying to flag down a car. A white man stopped, but when Daddy said he needed somebody to take his little girl to the doctor, he drove off."

I remember:

I am in the desert for the first time. I fall totally in love with it. I am so overwhelmed by its beauty, I confront for the first time, consciously, the meaning of the doctor's words years ago: "Eyes are sympathetic. If one is blind, the other will likely become blind too." I realize I have dashed about the world madly, looking at this, looking at that, storing up images against the fading of the light. *But I might have missed seeing the desert!* The shock of that possibility—and gratitude for over twenty-five years of sight—sends me literally to my knees. Poem after poem comes—which is perhaps how poets pray.

On Sight

I am so thankful I have seen
The Desert
And the creatures in the desert
And the desert Itself.

The desert has its own moon
Which I have seen
With my own eye.

There is no flag on it.
Trees of the desert have arms
All of which are always up
That is because the moon is up

The sun is up
Also the sky
The stars
Clouds
None with flags.

If there were flags, I doubt
the trees would point.
Would you?

> *But mostly, I remember this:*

I am twenty-seven, and my baby daughter is almost three. Since her birth I have worried about her discovery that her mother's eyes are different from other people's. Will she be embarrassed? I think. What will she say? Every day she watches a television program called "Big Blue Marble." It begins with a picture of the earth as it appears from the moon. It is bluish, a little battered-looking, but full of light, with whitish clouds swirling around it. Every time I see [it] I weep with love, as if it is a picture of Grandma's house. One day when I am putting Rebecca down for her nap, she suddenly focuses on my eye. Something inside me cringes, gets ready to try to protect myself. All children are cruel about physical differences, I know from experience, and that they don't always mean to be is another matter. I assume Rebecca will be the same.

But no-o-o-o. She studies my face intently as we stand, her inside and me outside her crib. She even holds my face maternally between her dimpled little hands. Then, looking every bit as serious and lawyerlike as her father, she says, as if it may just possibly have slipped my attention: "Mommy, there's a *world* in your eye." (As in, "Don't be alarmed, or do anything crazy.") And then, gently, but with great interest: "Mommy, where did you *get* that world in your eye?"

For the most part, the pain left then. (So what, if my brothers grew up to buy even more powerful pellet guns for their sons and to carry real guns themselves. So what, if a young "Morehouse man" once nearly fell off the steps of Trevor Arnette Library because he thought my eyes were blue.) Crying and laughing I ran to the bathroom, while Rebecca mumbled and sang herself off to sleep. Yes indeed, I realized, looking into the mirror. There *was* a world in my eye. And I saw that it was possible to love it: that in fact, for all it had taught me of shame and anger and inner vision, I *did* love it. Even to see it drifting out of orbit in boredom, or rolling up out of fatigue, not to mention floating back at attention in excitement (bearing witness, a friend has called it), deeply suitable to my personality, and even characteristic of me.

That night I dream I am dancing to Stevie Wonder's song "Always" (the name of the song is really "As," but I hear it as "Always"). As I dance, whirling and joyous, happier than I've ever been in my life, another bright-faced dancer joins me. We dance and kiss each other and hold each other through the night. The other dancer has obviously come through all right, as I have done. She is beautiful, whole and free. And she is also me.

QUESTIONS TO CONSIDER

1. What are some of the feelings that Alice Walker's family was not able to "see" in regards to her accident?

2. How does Alice Walker describe her relationship with her schoolmates before and after the surgery on her eye?

3. Who is able to see and appreciate Walker's blue eye?

Washington Park

BY ROBERT B. STEPTO

*The personal world of Robert Stepto is filled with rich family oral
narratives and ancestral voices that have been carefully preserved
for many generations. The son of a prominent Chicago physician
and accomplished music teacher, Stepto writes skillfully of his
long family history of middle-class privilege that has not been
immune from racism and disappointment. A professor of English
and Afro-American Studies at Yale University, Robert Stepto is the
author of* From Behind the Veil: A Study of Afro-American
Narrative *and co-editor of* Chant of Saints: A Gathering of
Afro-American Literature, Art and Scholarship. *This selection
is from* Blue as the Lake: A Personal Geography *(1998).*

My grandparents' place on Indiana Avenue was
indeed a house; a tidy, narrow, two-story brick affair
with a limestone face to the street, with a wall in common with the house next door that was a mirror image
of our house in terms of stairs, porch, windows, floor
plan, and most everything else. Their place was indeed
a house because, as my mother tells it, her mother insisted upon it: she was tired of living with her sister at 4545

Vincennes, a common enough arrangement for migrants to any big city—but an arrangement for how long? She was probably thinking, too, that if she was in Chicago to stay, and it was looking more and more that way, then she might as well begin to approximate in Chicago the house and household she had established in St. Joseph, Missouri, twenty years before. Of course, there wouldn't be the chickens, but maybe there could be much of what had been relinquished when Ocie, her husband, realized that even before the age of thirty he had exhausted his prospects in their hometown of St. Joe, despite or maybe *because* of his college degree.

So they moved to Chicago and later to Washington Park, timing matters, ordering their lives as family, church, Spelman, and Tuskegee[1] had taught them to do. It was no mere coincidence that they began to save and plan for a move right after my mother was born (they knew full well that you do not raise *three* children in someone else's house), or that they were poised to move right after Ocie received his pharmacy degree from Illinois and right before Anna (my mother) was to enter elementary school. When they moved they bought; and what they bought was a house with a garage opening out onto an alley where you could trade with the ice man, the rags 'n' old iron man, the vegetable man; a house with a bare narrow yard that my wife and I later would have strained to cultivate into a restful city garden, but which was for them a functional rectangle, suitable for burning trash at one end and for hanging clothes to dry at the other.

My grandparents bought their home from Germans who were master furniture makers, and who were slightly confused about why they had to sell and move no sooner than they had attained America—or better, why they had to move in order to maintain a certain

---

[1] Spelman and Tuskegee—historic black colleges.

citizenship in Chicago and America. Once the negotiations with the Germans were done, my grandparents finally had a Chicago house of their own, and two fine-crafted chairs in the bargain. I would like to think that the chairs, which are still in our family, were gifts of goodwill and housewarming. That's a good story. But the more significant one is the one my mother tells of the day, fifty years later, when my grandmother's eyes lit upon the chairs—after childrearing and householding, after Idlewild,[2] after the death of Ocie—and said, "The chairs; is this *all* that is left?"

Our immediate neighbors to the north and south were, like Grandpa Burns and most everybody else I knew of that generation, black postal workers, loyal both to the NAACP[3] and to the Republican party. To call their names and ours is like sounding the roster of an NBA basketball team, or like whispering that of a Yale secret society of yore, for we all had names like Collins and Kelly, Brown and Burns, York and Bush. We knew the Kellys best: the parents were kind and jovial, their sons both brilliant and destined for extremes of livelihood well beyond the steady rote of family, church, and modest **sinecure**.[4] One boy would prove gifted in mathematics and earn advanced degrees in that field despite the major obstacles the University of Chicago and the field itself would put before him. The other son was equally smart but far more social, streetwise, and slick; he was "into" "politics." When I saw him last he was **dapper**[5] and clean, wearing a little moustache and a good suit, and looking much too much like a younger version of my father. Last I heard, he was about to do time for some political "**impropriety**"[6]—unusual but

---

[2] Idlewild—African-American resort town in Michigan.

[3] NAACP—National Association for the Advancement of Colored People, a U.S. civil rights organization begun in 1909.

[4] **sinecure**—paying job that requires little work or effort.

[5] **dapper**—neat in appearance.

[6] **impropriety**—incorrectness.

nonetheless possible in Chicago, especially if one has crossed the wrong person in the ward or down at City Hall.

One neighbor was different from the rest of us. He had a big car, possibly a boat, and when he came home from wherever he worked he paraded around in "sport clothes," which told all that he had *not* come home to fix something or burn trash or stoke a furnace. I know he wasn't a postal worker, and I think maybe he was a milkman: they seemed to have a whole lot of style in the early 1950s, probably because they were delivering something in addition to milk. This man was bouncy, happy, and possession-laden; that's why he bought a big Doberman pinscher, to help him protect his stash.[7] This was seen in the neighborhood as both a necessary act (hence, on some level, to be forgiven) and an act of enormous **hubris**.[8] Down at Mr. Harris's barber shop, certain Negroes were saying things like: "The next thing that [expletive] is goin' do is go to *France* and marry hisself the onliest *Chinese* woman he can find!"

This neighbor—let us call him Mr. Simms—loved his Doberman and his Doberman loved him back. They would go through all sorts of paramilitary exercises in Simms's version of the spare backyard we all had; grandstanding, really, quaking the neighbors who merely wanted to take down wash or wax a car—or simply sit a bit without a whole lot of foolishness going on. Another thing Simms and the dog did was to prance down Indiana Avenue to the newsstand every waking morning, scattering schoolchildren like leaves before a blower, and some adults, too. On the way back, much was the same, only now the Doberman delicately held the morning paper in his huge jaws while Simms smirked like a circus lion tamer.

---

[7] stash—property or possessions.

[8] **hubris**—arrogance.

This and other things Simms was up to clearly communicated the following: "I got me a Doberman, got him trained, mess with me and you got much Dog up your [expletive]." People respected that; Simms's house was never approached, let alone robbed. But they were also incensed: for Simms's notion of the Protecting Dog was really that of the Harassing Dog, and that made Simms resemble a cracker sheriff[9] more than anything else, and more than he, all vibrant in his sport clothes, ever realized. Perhaps that's why the following story was told and softly chuckled over many times in my boyhood.

One morning, Simms was late for work and hadn't time for the prance to and from the corner newsstand. He carefully explained this to the Doberman, in just the way serious dog owners talk to their animals, and then went off to work. When he came home that night to a dark house, Simms turned on a light and called out the dog's name, eager to see his best friend. But there was no response, no leaping, licking greeting. Simms went into another room, switched on a light; called. Nothing. Then he went into a third room, called, and before he could flick the light switch, the [expletive] dog leapt from the dark into Simms's face, and bit Simms's ear off.

Just up the avenue from us was 58th Street, and the short stretch of 58th from Indiana Avenue east to Prairie to Calumet Avenue was an intense commercial district, brimming colorfully with every sort of store, business, and service. This was no doubt a result of the El[10] stop at 58th—stores have always sprouted around train stops of any kind—right between Prairie and Calumet. Some of the stores were members of chains: there was a Walgreen's drugstore at 58th and Prairie, and the other drugstore a block away at Indiana, Silberman's, was a

---

[9] cracker sheriff—offensive slang term for small town, southern, white, law enforcer.

[10] El—"elevated" train.

Rexall. But most of the enterprises were small, family or mom-and-pop affairs, with the usual breakdown of colored folk owning the barber and beauty shops, the rib joints, soulfood cafés and more than a few of the bars, while the whites ran the pharmacies, the hardware, dry goods, and grocery stores, the meat and fish markets. A few of these places are as memorable to me as are the houses I have lived in.

Silberman's was a dark, narrow place that was rather uninviting. My father had his first office in the **warren**[11] of rooms on the second floor. When Mr. Silberman retired he sold his business to a black employee—that was a breakthrough and a great and good thing. The Walgreen's was ordinary enough but stood out then as now for me because of its lunch counter. It was there, usually while out on a romp with my mother or Aunt Marge, that I would be treated to a frothy milk shake or to my favorite out-of-the-house sandwich, grilled ham on raisin toast. The counter was run by two or three foxy brownskin ladies, breathtaking even in uniforms and hairnets. Sisters like that naturally inspired a lot of fast talk—and Lord did they know how to dish it back. The banter at the lunch counter was funny, saucy, memorable; not as dirty as what came down at the barber shop, but still very adult.

When the lunch counter sit-ins began a few short years later in the South, and I watched the news films of the clubbings and draggings, the smearings of mustard and catsup, the burnings with lit cigarettes, my horror was matched only by my shame, the haunting shame of privilege. Nothing my elders ever said about privileges and "being grateful" cut half as deep as what I felt when I recognized that all I knew about lunch counters before 1958 was sweet talk and pretty ladies.

---

[11] **warren**—maze; network.

. . .

After I moved with my parents to our own house in Woodlawn, I would return to the old neighborhood for haircuts and church. Church in the beginning was Good Shepherd—the Church of the Good Shepherd; later, around the age of nine or ten, I attended St. Edmund's, more formally known as St. Edmund's King & Martyr.

Good Shepherd had formed in the late 1920s right around the corner from my grandparents' home on Indiana Avenue. Grandma and Grandpa Burns had joined Good Shepherd right after moving to the neighborhood, and thus were members of the church from its inception. This always struck me as being curious since Good Shepherd is Congregationalist (now, United Church of Christ) and they were raised as Baptists and had been reinforced in that faith by their experiences at Tuskegee and Spelman. When I finally asked my mother about this, she explained that when their parents had come to Chicago, they had joined one of the famous, established Baptist churches, Olivet (they were among the five thousand black migrants who, according to James Grossman,[12] joined Olivet between 1916 and 1919). But there had been a "falling out," something to do with "disrespect" at the time of my grandmother's sister's death. There may have been other reasons as well; at any rate, by the time I was born, Good Shepherd had been our church for almost twenty years. I was baptized there; it is the church to which the family returns to bury its dead, half wondering with no small degree of shame whether we can get home before getting mugged.

St. Edmund's is Episcopal and was my father's family's church. Indeed, my grandfather, Pa Step, had once been a member of the **vestry**:[13] somewhere I have

---

[12] James Grossman—contemporary American historian who writes about African-American migration from the South during the 1920s.

[13] **vestry**—committee elected by church members.

a photo of him almost glaring at the camera while at a board meeting, as I also have a photo of my father in his acolyte[14] years replete with cassock, surplice,[15] and a puffy bow at his neck. In its early years, St. Edmund's had no church building; its services and meetings were held in rooms at the Wabash YMCA. By the 1950s, however, the parish had grown and prospered: in buildings once occupied by a Greek Orthodox church at 61st and Michigan, we had both a church and an elementary school.

St. Edmund's was not just Episcopal but high church, something that was mischievously explained as a trace of Father Martin's former days as a Roman Catholic. We had "bells and smells" in abundance, "exotic" images on the walls and in the architecture left over from the Greek Orthodox days, a choir that knew how to turn everybody on with its mix of Bach and spirituals. We had the usual assemblage of **trifling**,[16] cigarette-sneaking acolytes who (myself included) nonetheless showed up every Sunday and actually knew the mass. I was confirmed into the Episcopal Church at St. Edmund's in June in 1957; Grandma and Grandpa Burns gave me as a present the Bible I still have. I doubt they would have been so congratulatory if they had known that I had become, not so much through coaching as through sheer self-invention, a "confirmed" Anglo-Catholic, deeply suspicious of Roman Catholics and Protestants alike. My days with them at Good Shepherd were just that far behind me.

How this came about—and why I was abruptly moved from Good Shepherd to St. Edmund's in the first place—is something I have tried to piece together. The family line on this is that I was moved because the

---

[14] acolyte—one who assists a priest or minister at certain religious services; an altar boy.

[15] cassock, surplice—garments worn by clergy.

[16] **trifling**—careless, indifferent.

Sunday School at Good Shepherd was lousy, nonexistent. There is some truth to this: all I can remember of Good Shepherd's Sunday School is the softball games. This is because during one of those games I received the Revelation that left-handed people are supposed to bat from the *other* side of the plate. (With that knowledge, and a little practice, my batting average went up a zillion points.) At St. Edmund's, by contrast, those rooms in the elementary school were put to *use* on Sundays: we had Sunday School and homework, too.

The family line makes sense but is too pat an answer: What more were we leaving behind, what else were we moving to? Why would my mother leave the church of her youth and join St. Edmund's? Why did I accept the move so easily—is it possible that I may have even initiated it? Two stories seem to bear on this.

It was late on a wintry Saturday afternoon; Good Shepherd's Cub Scout pack, of which I was a member, was returning to the city after a joyous day of tobogganing out in the western suburbs. Suddenly, the church bus pulled to the side of the road right in front of a hamburger joint. We were going to have a treat! Visions of milk shakes and french fries danced in my head.

The scoutmaster got off the bus and went in to see if it would be "all right." We all knew that "all right" wasn't simply about whether twenty Cub Scouts could enter the premises; it was about whether twenty black boys who claimed to be Scouts should be let in. When the scoutmaster returned, he spoke to us like this: "Now boys, we are going to go in here and have ourselves a sandwich or something. But I can tell you the people in there are none too pleased about all this. Now, I needn't *remind* you that we are *not* on the South Side of Chicago; this is *not* the chicken shack down the street from your house—do you follow me? Good, so I needn't *remind* you of how to BEHAVE, right? Am I right? OK; OK, now; let's go." With that, we filed off the bus, hitting each other whenever someone thought someone else was talking too loud.

The scene inside the hamburger place was not good. The white cook and counterman (both of whom looked like they should be sitting outside a filling station in Alabama) had instantly discovered, once deep into serving a bunch of Negroes, how much that disgusted them. They scowled, they muttered, they turned redder and redder by the minute. They half-cooked the food, threw it on a plate, and hurled the plate in almost anyone's direction. They clearly wanted us to leave, but in their fury constantly got the food orders wrong. We stayed, waiting for our food, perhaps out of conviction but more likely out of a kind of politeness (after all, the scoutmaster said, "BEHAVE"); witness for the first time in our lives to the spectacle of white men becoming unglued because of race. Then I said, loud enough and to no one—hence, to all: "Gee, this place has lousy service." No one replied; it was as if no one had heard me; but I had been heard.

When we got back on the bus, the scoutmaster started up: "You boys did fine in there. You all were real gentlemen. That is, all of you but one. I *asked* if you all knew how to behave, and you all said you did. Well, one of you *doesn't* know, and it's going to be a long time before I take *any* of you anywhere again." I honestly wondered who this terrible person was; who had brought this down on the whole Scout pack? I tried to recall if someone had been loud in the restaurant, or otherwise cut the fool. Had anybody not used their silverware, their napkin? Had someone forgotten to say "please" or "thank you" or "yes sir"? I knew I hadn't.

But the bad egg was me, and the scoutmaster in effect both listed my sins and had them posted. I was told that I had made a bad situation worse, and that if I had held my tongue the situation might have gotten better. I was told that I had endangered all of us, and had risked bringing violence upon us. I was told in pungent, quite **vernacular**[17] terms that I knew nothing about "facing adversity with **stoic**[18] dignity." I wanted to retort [Expletive!] I wanted to remind everyone of who took us in that "cracker café" in the first place, instead of waiting until we were back in Chicago. I wanted to scream, but I said nothing, and not even a scream came out. I just sat and took it, my cheeks burning, my body shrinking, tucking itself into the folds of my winter parka, into the darkness enveloping the bus as day so gratefully became night.

Soon the bus cranked up, and we were on our way. No one spoke to me, but I was consoled by the quickening certainty that we were no longer stalled in the suburbs and that being home was somehow going to happen. But we had an accident on the way home—a minor one—but accident enough. I am sure that there were some people on that bus who thought "This would not have happened if Stepto hadn't queered[19] the whole day for us." My thought was, "This is happening because we were so . . . **servile**."[20] We were a long time getting home.

After the episode in the suburbs, I was at best an indifferent Scout. I stopped doing the chores and projects that would earn me merit badges. I began to "play hooky" from Scout meetings, finding great pleasure in inventing places to go and in **coercing**[21] a Scout or two to go with me. Once we rode to the end of the line of the commuter train I usually used merely to go from one point to another within Chicago; we went to "see what we could see" and were bitterly disappointed to sight nothing of interest. Another time we went downtown to the Loop to a coffee shop famous for its hamburgers—

---

[17] **vernacular**—everyday speech.

[18] **stoic**—calm, unemotional.

[19] queered—spoiled, ruined.

[20] **servile**—humble; submissive.

[21] **coercing**—forcing.

I see now that that was a brave attempt to undo or revise what had happened in the suburbs after tobogganing. I continued as a Scout because I had a few friends, liked the uniform, and had no idea of how to act upon the emotions washing over me. So, too, did I value being in a context where I had an identity: at Good Shepherd and even in the Cub Scouts I was "Miss Burns's grandchild." I thought that was my best merit badge, and I thought everybody thought so as well, but that was before the Sunday Grandma was hooted in the large basement room where Sunday School was held, and I had to witness the spectacle.

I was outside the church playing softball. It had been a long time since any adult had suggested that Sunday School ought to foster something other than ball games, and so I was surprised when our game was broken up, and astonished by everything in the manner of the adult corraling us that told us we had been up to no good. When we arrived back inside the Sunday School area, there was much disarray and tension; the games and crafts which customarily occupied the youngsters not playing softball had been interrupted as well. People were grumbling: "What's going on?" "Who says this ain't a Sunday School?" "Sunday School these days ain't nothing but day care any way." "Somebody better wake up!" "I bet you one of them old-timey sisters from one of the guilds is behind this." "Who's that over there, passing out lessons?" "These children ain't going for none of that." "Who'd you say? Miss Burns? Oh, Lord, she done come back and doing it to us again."

The nut-brown woman with a determined look on her face, who was furiously slapping down lesson books (with Gentle Jesus on the cover) on top of board games and crayon drawings, was indeed "Miss Burns," my grandmother. I was **mortified**[22] but also confused: I hated the way she was calling attention to herself (and

---

[22] **mortified**—greatly embarrassed.

hence, so I thought, to me); I hated what most everyone was saying about her (but knew that I had thought those things, especially those times when she abruptly turned off the television, because the cowboy movie I was watching was "too violent"). Matters did not improve during the excruciating remaining minutes of the Sunday School hour. Most of the youngsters were, I would say, disrespectfully silent; most of the erstwhile Sunday School teachers made it *look* like they were up to something **pedagogical**.[23] Meanwhile, my grandmother, from her perch near the upright piano, sternly surveyed the scene, looking ever so much like your worst nightmare of a school principal or a plant manager.

Twenty minutes later, it was over, or almost over: Grandma had another card to play: she insisted that we revive the custom of ending Sunday School with a rousing rendition of "Onward, Christian Soldiers," which would end with all of us youngsters marching single-file out of the church building, gloriously into the sunshine. There was no recourse, especially after Grandma sat down at the upright and blanketed the room with hymnal chordings. The way out was simply the doorway through which we were to march, and march we did, though our clatter was hardly soldierlike. Once out into the sunshine, we wandered about, meandering in circles and half circles, trying to get a compass fix on our whereabouts. What I realized, once I got my bearings, was that I was in a zone of strange contradictions: I was outside the church when I was supposed to be inside; I was outside because my good Christian grandmother had in some real sense marched me outside; moreover, she had marched me outside in order to bring me, among others, inside—to make us true inhabitants of the church. It was all very confusing, wrenchingly so; I was quiet and subdued the rest of the day—I needfully got lost in a book, knowing well enough that this wasn't

---

[23] **pedagogical**—having to do with teaching.

a good day for testing the limits on *The Lone Ranger*. All this occurred in the spring, in May I think. By the fall I was a regular in the pews at St. Edmund's.

I was last at Good Shepherd a few years ago for my Aunt Marge's funeral. It was blisteringly hot, so much so that when we found out to our great dismay that the air-conditioning in the church had broken down that afternoon, a few family members just stayed in the cool of the rented limousines until the service began. I was exceedingly uncomfortable but too restless to sit in a limo; I needed to explore what I could of the church, revisiting the vast basement room where the Cub Scouts had met, and from which I had marched to the strains of "Onward, Christian Soldiers" into another boyhood. I also needed to get a closer look at the children across the street, playing in the spray of an opened fire hydrant. Would they mind? Would they let me get close enough to see if I could see my child self in them? The heat bore in, I needed to get back in one of the limos, but I wanted more to walk around to the 57th Street side of the church to scrutinize the lot (really, the church's backyard) where I had played so many outdoor games, and learned to hit a softball, too. It was much as I thought it would be: narrow, spare, scruffy; I must have been a little tyke indeed to have once considered it a suitable space for serious ball games.

Then it occurred to me: you're already on 57th Street, maybe a quarter of the way to Grandma's house, why don't you walk down the street and around the corner and have a look? The appropriateness of this could not be disputed. To see the Burns house would be to see where our Washington Park life had begun sixty years before, and where my life had begun just after World War II. Even from across the street, I would be able to examine the little side entrance to the basement apartment where Marge and Rog had lived, and to watch the fading August sun burnish the second-floor window of what had been my parents' room, and later my room whenever I overnighted with my grandparents. I thought that all I was trying to pull together by roaming around instead of being in the limo would instantly **coalesce**[24] once on Indiana Avenue, once reading the house numbers, "5722."

But I didn't go around the corner, even though I ventured seven or eight steps toward it. This was not because I thought I might miss the beginning of the service or because it was too hot to amble the streets. I didn't go because I was too well dressed and too light skinned; because I had a little money in my pocket and because I was wearing the nice watch my wife gave me for our twentieth anniversary. One side of my brain said, "Hey, my man, you're a brother—go on down to your grandmother's house and check it out." The other side said, "Don't fall for that romantic [expletive]; this neighborhood has *changed*; walk two blocks and you're a dead man; the next funeral at Good Shepherd will be yours." Perhaps because a woman had been mugged at the wake the night before—she came running back into the Church screaming, "My purse's been taken, he took my purse!" as if any of us could do anything about it— I listened to the second voice in my head. But I was angered by what was preventing me, a former child of those streets, from doing anything I wanted. So, too, was I angry about not being able to make the connection, which I thought to be the best possible connection, with the people, sites, and images that would put my life in order.

But I was wrong, for when I finally quit gazing down the street I wouldn't walk and entered the church, I found a feast for my eyes: the much older but still quite recognizable **visage**[25] of the scoutmaster who had taken

---

[24] **coalesce**—unite, come together.

[25] **visage**—facial expression.

us tobogganing and later **pilloried**[26] me some thirty-five years before. Family and friends from the year one broached conversation, and I believe I engaged them. But my eye was on Mr. B. Later I approached him, reminded him of how we knew each other, asked him how he had been, asked after his son, whom I remembered to be the Willie Mays of Cub Scouts. Mr. B. was very good at assisting the minister with the service, very short on everything else. He didn't remember me, and I almost got the feeling that he didn't remember the son of whom I had inquired.

This and the fact that, when it was time for me to speak, I was actually introduced as a *friend* of the family, and not as family, not as the firstborn nephew of the woman we were burying, made me aware not just of the **corrosive**[27] forces of time, but also of what the young put in place to create chasms between the generations. I had wanted to be shut of Good Shepherd, and thirty-five years later I was faced with the evidence of how well I had succeeded.

---

[26] **pilloried**—ridiculed, scolded.

[27] **corrosive**—causing deterioration.

QUESTIONS TO CONSIDER

1. "Gee this place has lousy service." Why was this a dangerous statement for Stepto to make in a white restaurant during the 1950s?

2. How does Stepto describe his grandmother's performance as the "Sunday School Matron"?

3. Why do you think Stepto's return to his old neighborhood is so painful?

from

Unafraid of the Dark

BY ROSEMARY L. BRAY

"Do you know that you are the kind of student a teacher waits his whole life to teach?" Those words, spoken to Rosemary Bray by her white eighth-grade teacher at Francis Parker School, gave her the courage and self-confidence to continue her educational journey to become one of the first black women at Yale. Living between two worlds is a central theme in Bray's memoir, Unafraid of the Dark *(1985). In it, she describes growing up poor in Chicago in the 1960s, and her daily childhood travels from her home, which is strained by poverty and family tension, to the "storybook" world of wealth and access. Bray is a former editor of the* New York Times Review of Books *and an author of a children's biography of Martin Luther King, Jr.*

One day when I came home from school, Mama and Daddy were talking in Daddy's room. For once they seemed more curious than **antagonistic**[1] toward each other. Mama asked me how I felt about the idea of going to a new school. It would be far away from where we lived, and I would have to take a train to the North Side of Chicago by myself, she said. Right away my ten-year-old's spirit of adventure was kindled. The idea of doing anything by myself was a small miracle.

It seemed that my mother had told our caseworker that we were all doing well in school, but that she was worried about me. The kids were still picking on me every day and Mama still had to meet me after school. What's more, the nuns were just as concerned but for different reasons. I needed a bigger challenge, according to my sixth-grade teacher, Sister Maria Sarto, one she felt I might get at another school with more money and resources. There were several such schools in Chicago, but the big requirement was a scholarship to pay for my going there. At least one of those places was a boarding school, which I was more than ready for. But neither of my parents was ready for that step. I was too young to be away from home, they said. My mother was especially appalled; in her mind, boarding school was where white people sent their children to get them out of the way.

So the caseworker had found out about this other school, the Francis W. Parker School, and had brought my mother the application form. She told Mama to fill out the application and send it back to the school. I looked at it and knew I would have to be the one to fill it out. It didn't take long to do, and a few weeks after we mailed it we were notified that I would have to take some kind of test before a decision could be made. I didn't mind that. Not long after, I found myself in a big

---

[1] **antagonistic**—hostile, unfriendly.

room with a lot of kids, filling in those computer-scored blank ovals. I was too excited to pay real attention to how few black people were in the room. My mind was on getting to go to this school. It was something I could do without the constant presence of my **siblings**,[2] without people making fun of me all the time, something that was mine alone.

On Holy Saturday, the day before Easter, a letter came in the mail from Parker. My mother let me open it; I had been accepted. I screamed and ran through the house. My brothers and sister gawked; my parents grinned at each other in a rare show of united pleasure. What I didn't know for many years was that Sister Maria Sarto had called the school and spoken to the principal and some of the teachers about me. One of the teachers she spoke to that day would make a terrific difference in my life a few years later. But all I knew at the time was that I had done something that was an honor for the family.

Not long after, they sent a list of the clothes I would need; though the school was **nonsectarian**,[3] I would still be wearing uniforms. But these were not the ugly blue-and-green plaid of the parochial school. These were quieter colors, solid navy blue and white, with light-blue blouses or knee socks allowed. Mama and I scrounged through thrift shops all summer, looking for skirts to cut down for me. For the first day of school, however, we found something special. It was a light-blue dress—a woman's dress—lavishly embroidered with flowers of every imaginable color and intertwined with leaves and stems of forest green. I thought it was the most perfect, pretty thing I ever saw. It even had a big skirt to swish when I twirled around in it. Mama bought it and cut it down for me to wear, tucking in the sides and waist with her old Singer pedal sewing machine.

---

[2] **siblings**—brothers and sisters.

[3] **nonsectarian**—not joined to a religion.

On the morning of the first day of school, Mama went with me, and cautioned me to pay close attention. She would go with me the whole way this first time; after that, I had to go each day alone. I was eleven; it was thrilling. We walked to Forty-seventh Street and took the bus to the El. That part was familiar; I had been this way on trips downtown. Then we gave the attendant our transfers so she could punch and return them and climbed the long stairs to the elevated platform. Mama reminded me to always say "Return, please," to hold on to my transfer until I was on the Clark Street or Broadway bus. Transfers were good for an hour in Chicago; you could ride buses and trains in any order as often as you wanted, until your time ran out. That's why it was important to look at the time punched on the little transfer clock. The trip to school would take just about an hour, and bus drivers routinely gave you a little more time.

On the train, I stood at the little window up front, just as I would have if I'd been going anywhere with Mama, and watched as the tracks descended into the caverns under downtown Chicago. I counted the stops as I always did: Roosevelt Road, Harrison, Jackson and State, Madison-Monroe and State, Randolph and State. That was as far as I'd ever gone on the El until recently. The train took an enormous screeching turn; the sparks flew from the wheels of the train and sputtered out. Then we were pulling into the stations new to me: Grand and State; Chicago and State. Finally, Mama tapped me on the shoulder and told me our stop was next. Clark and Division was painted red; that was how I would teach myself to remember where to get off the train until it became automatic. We went through the turnstiles, and walked up the stairs into the open fall air.

The sun was shining that day; the streets looked so clean you could eat from them. And in contrast to the handful of rugged, slightly rundown stores that occupied Forty-third and Forty-seventh Streets near our house, this intersection was overrun with stores: shoe shops and restaurants, a huge Woolworth's, a jewelry store. The street was full of people, not the slow procession of my neighbors headed for the store or the bus stop, but a steady, vigorous stream of people going—it seemed—everywhere.

Mama directed me to walk across the street and stand at the bus stop. I could take a 22 or a 36 bus, and both of them would stop where I wanted to go. The school was at Clark and Webster, she said, and I could ask the driver to stop at Webster. Or I could get off at Belden, the next stop, and walk back a half-block. We rode past high-rise buildings in formation, and townhouses that looked like cleaned-up versions of our own building. Soon we rode past another private school, the Latin School, which I would learn later was Parker's **archrival**.[4] The bus ride gave me my first glimpse of Lincoln Park, and I wondered where the famous zoo was to be found. It turned out to be in back of the school; the zoo's entrance was right across the street from the football field.

Soon my mother buzzed for the bus to stop, and we got off across the street from a low, sprawling brick structure, with lots of windows, a courtyard with trees, two playgrounds, and a huge playing field. The signs directed us to the front entrance, a set of stairs with a driveway in front and a low brick wall running the length of the property. As Mama and I came up the steps, I could hear the buzz of children's voices. When we reached the top and peered through the windows, I saw a huge space filled with children and teenagers. I was **incredulous**:[5] there were hundreds of kids there, and every one of them, it seemed to me, was white.

No one had told me. They had talked about what a good school it was. They had talked about what a

---

[4] **archrival**—major rival.

[5] **incredulous**—disbelieving.

wonderful thing it would be for me to come here; they had talked about how many more interesting things I would be able to do here. Not one soul—not even my parents—had thought to mention a crucial detail. I would be going to school with white people, and anyone with an ounce of sense knew white people were dangerous.

I literally backed away from the door. "Mama, those people are white!" I couldn't believe she looked so unexcited. "They'll kill me!" She watched the same news I watched; she knew white people had thrown bricks at us in the demonstrations in Chicago years earlier. She knew as well as I did that white people **sicced**[6] dogs on little boys in Selma and blew up churches in Birmingham[7] while little girls were in Sunday school and shot people in the back in Mississippi and nearby Cicero and spit on them everywhere. Now she wanted me to go to school with them? What could she and Daddy have been thinking about?

Mama took my hand and pulled me through the door. "Girl, these kids ain't going to bother you. You're here to get an education." We walked inside to the near center of the hall. What looked like chaos had its own curious sense of order. What seemed to be a milling crowd was in fact a cluster of several grades, including my own. I was to be in Mrs. Reid's seventh-grade class. My mother found Mrs. Reid just in time; at eight A.M. the bell rang, and the crush of students began heading for stairs, some up, some down. I was headed down. I looked back helplessly at my mother. "I'll be up here," she said.

Inside the classroom, Mrs. Reid asked the new children to stand with her. The other new kids were boys; at least one of them was handsome; all of them looked as though they belonged there. The teacher

[6] **sicced**—urged to attack.
[7] Selma and Birmingham—Southern cities where black organized protests against segregation occurred in the 1950s.

asked for volunteers, seasoned students to act as guides for the newcomers. When my turn came, only one hand went up. It was attached to a thin girl with curly brown hair and braces; her name was Monica. I had no idea at the time that she was already as unpopular as I would become. When homeroom was dismissed, she came up to me and grabbed my hand, offering to show me around. By the time I located my mother, Monica already was leading me off to the library. "Look Mama, I have a friend," I said to her.

For a very long time, Monica was my only friend. I was fine in the classroom. The work was challenging, not hard, and there was always something interesting to do, a project you could make up for class. Monica and I both loved science, as it turned out. She and I both wanted to be doctors—not such a popular thing for eleven-year-old girls to want in the 1960s. But we were so weird no one was surprised.

I was surprised at the number of kids in my class who were Jewish. It might never have come up if it hadn't been for the fact that several of them were being confirmed or bar mitzvahed.[8] I had heard of confirmation; I'd been confirmed the previous year. But the solemn ceremony of the bar mitzvah was new to me. Monica wasn't going to be bas mitzvahed[9] but she was Jewish, too. I learned a lot that year about the High Holy Days and Jewish food (which it turned out my father knew all about from his **abortive**[10] attempts at restaurants). I learned about dreidels[11] and Purim[12] (which I loved because it involved one of my favorite characters from the Bible, Esther) and Yom Kippur.[13]

---

[8] bar mitzvahed—put through the religious rite of passage for a Jewish boy.

[9] bas mitzvahed—put through the religious rite of passage for a Jewish girl.

[10] **abortive**—short-lived; unsuccessful.

[11] dreidels—toys used during Hanukkah, a Jewish holiday.

[12] Purim—Jewish holiday.

[13] Yom Kippur—Jewish holiday.

I could appreciate the idea of having one day a year to confess every bad thing you'd done, as opposed to doing it continually, every Saturday afternoon, as Catholic kids did.

I also learned Jesus was a Jew. I cannot account for how it was that I missed that minor detail, but I did. When Monica pointed out the logic of it—how he had to be a Jew or they would never have called him Rabbi in certain parts of the New Testament—I was stunned. Monica and I were constantly having great debates over religion. We were much more preoccupied with it than with race. For a while, I kept trying to baptize her; I would wet my hands in the water fountain and chase her around the playground, reciting the words from the Baltimore Catechism:[14] "I baptize you in the name of the Father, and of the Son, and of the Holy Ghost."

But after going to my classmates' bar mitzvahs and seeing the solemnity and beauty of the ceremony (and looking at the astounding gifts they received afterward), and after long religious discussions with Monica, I decided that I should be Jewish too. My parents had a fit. My father said: "What, being black isn't trouble enough; you want to be a Jew too?" I realize now that my desire had more to do with wanting to be like my best friend, with wanting to belong, than it did with any kind of conversion experience. But it took a particular incident to make it clear to me just how much I didn't belong.

It was the afternoon I went to play with Susie Levitt after school. She had asked me over to play earlier in the week. Because I was under strict orders to come home directly from school, going to her house required special dispensation[15] from my parents, since I'd get home after dark. But Mama and Daddy seemed glad for once that I was making friends, and they'd agreed to let me go.

---

[14] Baltimore Catechism—the official text for the religious instruction of Catholic children in the United States until 1962.

[15] special dispensation—release from a holy law. The author is being funny.

I knew the way to her house from the address: I passed within a block of where she lived each morning. I got off the bus a bit earlier than I usually did, and walked around the corner onto a street of immaculate brownstones. When I reached her address, a narrow, five-story house, I climbed the stairs and was momentarily confused. I couldn't figure out which apartment was hers; there was only one bell, with no message about how many rings would signal her. I took a chance and rang the bell once, figuring someone would direct me to where she lived.

A white woman in a uniform answered the door. When I told how I had come to see Susie, she opened the door wider and let me inside. I looked around for the mailboxes in the **vestibule**;[16] there were none. I walked into the front room as Susie came downstairs. Something astounding dawned on me as we said hello: there were no apartments. The whole house was hers to live in. Susie asked if I wanted to see the house. I did. She took me through the parlor to the formal dining room and into the kitchen, where a black woman about my mother's age had her back to us. Susie asked me if I wanted a snack; I said no. The woman turned and smiled slightly at me and said hello. I said hello softly, then followed Susie out and upstairs. On the next level, another woman in uniform was ironing clothes as we passed. We walked up and up the elegant winding staircase until we reached the top floor, and Susie opened a door into what looked to me like Paradise.

In the life of every young girl, there is one fantasy. Some girls want the most beautifully dressed life-size doll. Others dream of a shining prince to take them away one day to live as his wise and beautiful queen. My fantasy was small: one day I would have my own room. I had never even given any thought to what

---

[16] **vestibule**—hallway; entry.

would be in the room; I just knew that one day I would have a room that no one was in but me. Susie already had such a room, but she had more. The room contained the decor of a little girl's dreams. Everything in it was white and gold: the dresser, the mirror frame, the vanity and most of all, the four-poster canopy bed. White curtains floated across the top, sheltering the bed like clouds.

I wanted to know where her brothers and sister slept. She cheerfully showed me her siblings' rooms— none the room of my dreams, but each separate and apart. I don't remember what we did that afternoon. I only remember feeling numb and vague. All the way home I replayed the scenes at her house. By the time I got to Forty-seventh Street to take the bus home, the contrast was evident. The noise of the train, the smells of barbecue from the shack across the street, the sporadic blare of Motown[17] in the record shop as customers checked to be sure the 45[18] they wanted to buy was the right one, the strolling people in late afternoon, all dark like me, all different from those who inhabited the world I'd left only forty-five minutes earlier. I was different, too.

I walked home from the bus stop, back down Ellis Avenue, past the tansy[19] growing in the cat lady's yard, past the blackberry bush, past Denise Young's fence. I turned on Forty-fifth Street, past the wisps of morning glory vines and the pods filled with next spring's seeds, across the alley to knock on the back door. Mama let me in and asked me if I'd had a good time. I said I had. What else could I say, when anything else would have worried her? Daddy wasn't home yet. I walked through to the front room and put down my school things, hung

---

[17] Motown—major African-American music company founded in Detroit in the 1950s.

[18] 45—small phonograph record popular in the 1950s; it turned at forty-five revolutions per minute.

[19] tansy—strong-smelling plant with yellow flowers and feathery leaves that are sometimes used in cooking.

up my coat. My sister and brothers were playing, Mama was cooking. I walked back to the bathroom, painted a year earlier a brilliant emerald-green enamel that I now saw emphasized the cracking walls. I shut the latch tight before I sat down on the toilet and started to cry.

Being black was not the worst of it; I realized that afternoon that I was poor, too. I would not have my own room, or a white-and-gold canopy bed. Suddenly it was clear—the way my blue skirts and white blouses looked and felt so different from the other girls'. The soft wool they wore did not come from Sears or Goldblatt's, but from Marshall Field or Saks Fifth Avenue. My blouses were not cotton, they were 100 percent drip-dry polyester. I didn't have penny loafers or Bass Weejuns. I had shoes from the 2-for-$5 store. I knew the facts of all these things long before; I had joined with my mother in planning around them. But this was the day I felt it—how different, how really different I was.

When I was cried out, I wiped my face over and over with cold water until I could pass for normal. Fortunately, no one had paid much attention to how long I'd been in the bathroom. They assumed I had started reading something and lost track of time, as I always did. They were wrong this time. Something in me had broken somehow, but I was determined that they wouldn't know. For them to know, it seemed to me, would mean they would feel bad. And I didn't want Mama or Daddy or anybody to feel bad. We couldn't help being poor. It wasn't anybody's fault. And if I hadn't started going to that school, I probably wouldn't even have known. But it was too late for me; I knew that now. And in the months that followed, except when I was with a couple of people like Monica, I grew more silent and unhappy in my awareness. Now I know the feeling for what it was. I was ashamed.

QUESTIONS TO CONSIDER

1. How would you describe the author's initial reaction to her new school?

2. What is the significance of Monica's relationship with Bray?

3. How are the author's and Monica's worlds different? Why does their difference shock Bray?

A Day with My Father

BY DANZY SENNA

What does it mean to be biracial in America? Danzy Senna explores this question in her first published novel Caucasia *(1998) which takes a look at the relationship between two sisters, one fair and the other brown-skinned, who are children of an interracial marriage. The characters in this selection travel a path similar to that taken by Senna, the daughter of a black father and a white mother, who grew up in Boston and eventually earned a Master of Fine Arts at the University of California at Irvine. In the following excerpt, the narrator, Birdie Lee, is out for a day in the park with her father in the 1970s. The scene demonstrates one of the ways in which issues of race entered her life.*

My father wouldn't come into the house. Ever since he had left us that bright July morning, he acted as if the house were contaminated. Cole and I told him that the visitors had disappeared, but still he refused to enter. Instead, he'd just honk outside and Cole and I would go tearing down the stairs together and out into his car.

My mother would watch from the window, a scowl set on her face, and I always felt a little guilty leaving her behind.

He usually came for us on Saturday mornings. Cole called it "Divorced Fathers Day." She said all her friends had them too. He'd take us to the Public Gardens if it was nice out, or to the Museum of Fine Arts if it was raining.

Sometimes, if we begged, he would take us to a movie—any kind, any rating, so we always made him take us to slasher films. Once there, he would wait for us in the lobby, reading a book on some obscure topic, while we shoveled popcorn and Jujyfruits down our throats and stared, glassy-eyed, at the horrors on the screen.

I can't say that I enjoyed these visits with my father. He never had much to say to me. In fact, he never seemed to see me at all. Cole was my father's special one. I understood that even then. She was his **prodigy**[1]— his young, gifted, and black. At the time, I wasn't sure why it was Cole and not me, but I knew that when they came together, I disappeared. Her existence comforted him. She was the proof that his blackness hadn't been completely blanched. By his four years at Harvard. By my mother's blue-blood family wedding reception in the back of the big rotting house on Fayerweather Street. By so many years of standing stiffly in corners, listening to those sweatered tow-haired preppies[2] talk about the Negro Problem, nursing their vermouth, glancing at him with so much pleased incredulity in their eyes. Those Crimson boys[3] with all their asinine questions, all their congratulatory remarks about how they saw him as different, had made him want to disappear. They saw

---

[1] **prodigy**—exceptionally talented youth.

[2] preppies—students of a private preparatory school.

[3] Crimson boys—Harvard University students.

him and all his seeming repose, his **sardonic**[4] smile, as evidence that the black race was indeed human. The very fact that they needed evidence made him **nauseous**.[5] But somehow, somewhere, he accepted the terms of their debate, and he spent years perfecting his irony and stale wit in order to distinguish himself from the poor black blokes scuttling around the outskirts of the city. Perfected it so well that when he finally returned to Wally's one night, a small jazz joint on Tremont Street, he imagined that the cluster of brown and yellow and black faces that dotted the smoky air were laughing at him, mocking his stiff posture and tight smile.

Cole was his proof that he had indeed survived the integrationist[6] shuffle, that he had remained human despite what seemed a conspiracy to turn him into stone. She was his proof of the pudding, his milk-chocolate pudding, the small dusky body, the burst of mischievous curls (nappier than his own), the full pouring lips (fuller than his own). Her existence told him he hadn't wandered quite so far and that his body still held the power to leave its mark.

He usually treated me with a cheerful disinterest— never hostility or ill will, but with a kind of impatient amusement, as if he were perpetually tapping his foot, waiting for me to finish my sentence so he could get back to more important subjects.

And strange as it may sound, I had never really been alone with my father. Not that I could remember, anyway. So when I got the chance that fall morning, I felt I was going on a blind date and went toward it jittery, with a mixture of hope and fear.

It wouldn't have happened at all if Cole hadn't gotten sick. It might have been just another outing, me in

---

[4] **sardonic**—scornful.

[5] **nauseous**—sick to his stomach; disgusted.

[6] integrationist—means of bringing races together.

the backseat, making cat's cradles with my string; Cole in the front, trying to listen to the radio and my father's lecture all at once. But that morning Cole claimed to have the flu, and it was too late to stop my father. He was already on his way over.

My mother stood up in our room, holding the back of her hand to Cole's forehead.

Cole sniffled and looked at me through red, watery eyes. "You go, Birdie." She was being very melodramatic about it, and my mother was buying it hook, line, and sinker. She had already gone out to buy Cole the latest issue of *Jet* and a box of cherry-flavored Sucrets, which Cole refused to share with me.

My mother nodded. "Yeah, baby. You go alone with your papa and have a good time."

I stared at my feet, then turned to go down to his car.

When I approached him, he looked up from his book quizzically, and then his eyes roamed behind me for Cole, the real reason he was here.

"Cole's not coming. She's sick," I told him. I stood beside his open window, hands shoved in my pockets, waiting to see if he'd call the whole thing off.

He squinted at the house suspiciously. He was always accusing my mother of trying to keep him from us—"us" meaning Cole.

"Sick with what?"

"A cold. Mum says she's got a fever."

"Hmmph."

Then he looked at me and smiled, a little shyly, I thought.

"Well, then it'll just be the two of us, Patrice. Right?" Sometimes, when he was being particularly affectionate, he would call me by my old name. This was a rarity, however. It meant he was making an extra-special effort to connect with me.

He was quiet as he drove us to the Public Gardens. It was a beautiful day outside, one of those late-fall days in New England when the ground is carpeted with colors, the sky a bright blank blue. My father was listening to the radio, the way he always did, head cocked to the side in thought, mouth turned down in concentration. It was the public radio station, and they were talking about the imprisonment of some radicals in California. I listened vaguely and chewed on my hair.

"Bird, you see much of that Redbone character around the house?"

I thought about it. I hadn't seen Redbone. But that didn't mean he hadn't been there. My mother's friends came over some Sundays for meetings in the basement. Usually, my mother would send us up to our room before they went down into the cavernous, mysterious basement.

"Nope. I haven't seen him. He's weird. I don't like him."

We were at a red light now, and my father was looking at me, seeming to ponder my features with a scientific interest. He ruffled my hair. "Well, you tell me if he comes around. I don't think your mother knows what she's gotten herself into. You know what I mean?"

I nodded, not really sure what he meant, but excited that we had an agreement. I would be his spy.

He switched the station then, and we listened to music the rest of the way over, singing along to the Stylistics, our voices rising and falling together, cracking at the high notes.

We wandered around the Public Gardens for a few hours, and though we didn't talk much, I felt closer to my father than I ever had before. We held hands and went on the swan rides together. There was a man selling T-shirts, and my father bought me one that said "Wet Paint" across the front in raised multicolored letters that dribbled down like real paint. He took a picture of me in my new T-shirt, worn over my long-sleeved one so that the long sleeves billowed out like a pirate's.

He bought a newspaper then and lay on the grass while I did cartwheels in circles around him. There were other families and couples scattered around, enjoying the unusually mild temperature and the fallen leaves. I think it was when he gave me a few dollars to buy us hot dogs that I noticed the couple. They were walking a dog—small gray terrier—they were older, well-dressed. The woman's hair was silvery blond. Her companion was a small and dour man wearing a trench coat and holding a cane. They watched me, frowning, as I went up to the hot-dog cart and made my purchase. The man had a fierce scowl, but the woman smiled slightly at me, so I smiled back. I thought maybe my fly was unzipped, but when I looked down, all was in place.

They continued to watch me as I brought the hot dog to my father, then ran back to the cart to get us napkins, which I had forgotten.

My father didn't seem to notice, so I put them out of my mind. After we finished our hot dogs, I lay with my head on his stomach, so that our bodies made a T. I read the funnies there, occasionally reading jokes aloud to him, which he ignored, but which I giggled at anyway.

When I was done with the funnies, I watched the sky—the shapes of animals made out of clouds. And when I tilted my head slightly to the side, I saw again that strange couple with their gray terrier, pointing at me. I didn't move, just watched it happen with a lazy interest. They were talking to two men in uniform, the police on their beat, and then the four of them were trudging across the grass in our direction.

I didn't move until they were nearly upon us. Then I sat up and nudged my father, who had begun to doze off.

He opened his eyes just as their shadow fell over him.

He sat up abruptly, and the two of us scrambled to our feet. My father did what he did when he was nervous: adjusted his glasses and cleared his throat.

One of the policemen was older, with a beer belly, and creases in his face that made him look angry, even if he wasn't. The other one was a younger guy, with dark hair and a mustache. He had laughing eyes but was trying to look serious.

The couple stood off to the distance slightly, petting their dog and whispering.

"All right, brotherman," the younger one said to my father with a smirk. "Who's the little girl?"

My father looked down at me and laughed slightly. "She's my daughter. Is there a problem?" His voice shook as he said it, and I could feel his fear from where I stood.

The older cop looked at me in my Wet Paint shirt over my long-sleeved one. I understood what was going on, even if I couldn't have explained it at the time, and my skin was tingling all over like the prickle of salt water when you stay in the ocean too long. I stared at the couple and had an urge to go over and kick dirt at them.

The cops didn't believe my father. Not even when he showed them a photograph of me and my sister that he kept in his wallet. Not even when he had shown them his identification card, which read, "Deck Lee, Associate Professor, Anthropology, Boston University." What made it worse was that people around us had begun to notice and had moved closer to see what was happening. They whispered among themselves, eyeing me with concern, and that made me feel ashamed.

I stood beside my father, and the policeman—the younger one with the mustache—leaned down and touched my hair in a way that made me flinch. He smiled, and said, "What's your name, kid?"

"Birdie."

"Birdie? That's a funny name. Now, why don't you tell me your real name?"

"Birdie Lee," I said it louder this time.

"All right, Birdie Lee. How do you know this man?"

He looked at my father, who was standing with the other cop. My father was staring at me with a tense smile.

"He's my father."

The cop laughed a little. Then he touched my shoulder and pulled me away from my father and the other cop, so we were leaning into each other. Secretive. He said in a whisper, "You can tell us, kiddie. He can't hurt you here. You're safe now. Did the man touch you funny?"

I felt sick and a little dizzy. I wanted to spit in the cop's face. But my voice came out quiet, whimpier than I wanted it to. "No, he didn't. He's my father" was all I could manage. I wondered what my sister would do. I figured she wouldn't be in this situation in the first place, and that fact somehow depressed me.

The cop seemed disappointed by my answer and stood up, shrugging with exasperation at his partner.

After grilling my father for a few more minutes, they left us alone. But the old couple didn't leave. They watched us as we gathered up our things, our strewn-about newspapers. As we walked the distance across the grass to our car, I turned to see them still watching us. I raised my middle finger and blew a kiss to the couple on it, the way I had seen the Irish kids do on television. I was about to shout something, too, when my father grabbed my arm roughly, pulling me to his side and quickening his pace. "Cut that . . . out" was all he said.

When we were in the car, my father buckled me into my seat belt. From his expression I could see that he didn't feel like talking. He played music on the way back. I knew all the words but decided not to sing along. He seemed deep in thought, and before he let me out in front of the house, he smiled at me, crookedly, sadly. "And they wonder why we want to get out of this place. I mean, . . . it's everywhere I go.

Everywhere." He stared at me for a moment, our eyes locked. Then he added, "Study them, Birdie. And take notes. Always take notes."

Usually he kissed me on the top of my head before he said good-bye, but this time he just touched my forehead with the back of his hand, as if he were checking for a fever. His own hand was cold, and he pulled it away quickly, as if the touch had burned him.

QUESTIONS TO CONSIDER

1. What do the suspicious couple in the park observe and fail to observe about Birdie and her father that leads them to call the police over?

2. Why does the police officer keep insisting that it is okay for Birdie to tell him the truth about her relationship with her father?

3. What do you think Birdie learns about race from the encounter with the police in the park?

Fighting for Freedom

Segregation By 1885 most southern states had segregated school systems and separate hotels, theaters and restaurants for black and white customers. In the 1896 *Plessy* v. *Ferguson* case, the Supreme Court accepted the "separate but equal" argument that permitted separate public facilities for blacks and whites.

▲
A young girl stands by a drinking fountain designated for blacks.

Martin Luther King, Jr. The civil rights leader heads a
1960s demonstration. ▶

Thurgood Marshall was a leading civil rights activist and the first African American to become a Supreme Court Justice. He successfully fought for the desegregation of public schools in 1954. ▶

National Association for the Advancement of Colored People
Founded in 1909, the NAACP is a civil rights organization in the United States that seeks to end discrimination against all people of color. It played a key role in passing the Civil Rights Acts of 1957 and 1964 and successfully campaigned for economic sanctions against South Africa in the 1980s. ▶

A member of the NAACP looks for support from a passerby.
▼

Recruiters in 1961 in New York City work to attract new members.

WE WANT BLACK POWER

▲
Malcolm X (1925–1965) A prominent member of the Nation of Islam, he vigorously supported civil rights for African Americans, often using militant rhetoric to get his point across. His struggle for civil rights was cut short by an assassin's bullet.

◀ **The Black Panther Party** This radical political organization sought to improve the treatment of blacks in society. Some in the group supported revolution in order to bring about social change.

▲

Barbara Jordan (1936–1996) One of the first African-American women to serve in Congress, she was a representative from Texas in the 1970s. Jordan was the keynote speaker at the Democratic National Convention in 1976.

Angela Davis One of the leaders of the Black revolution of the 1960s and 1970s, Davis worked with the SNCC (Student Nonviolent Coordinating Committee), the Black Panther Party, and the Communist Party. She is a noted scholar whose work focuses on gender and racial inequality and oppression. ▶

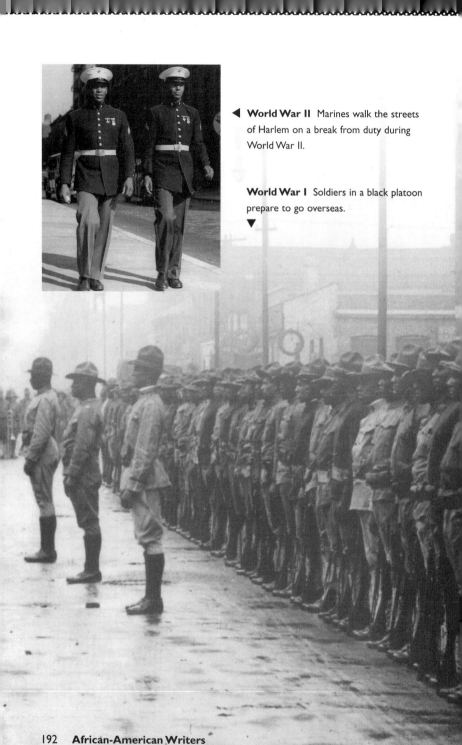

World War II Marines walk the streets of Harlem on a break from duty during World War II.

World War I Soldiers in a black platoon prepare to go overseas.
▼

◀ **Desert Storm** The first black officer to hold the nation's highest military post, chairman of the Joint Chiefs of Staff, Colin Powell played a pivotal role in planning and executing the Persian Gulf War.

Vietnam An African-American paratrooper leads a patrol in Vietnam in 1966.

▼

four

Fighting on Two Fronts: On Being Black and American

On Being Black and American

BY LANGSTON HUGHES AND W.E.B. DUBOIS

The 14th Amendment to the U.S. Constitution, passed in 1868, granted blacks citizenship and civil rights. The 15th Amendment, passed in 1870, guaranteed the right to vote to all male citizens. Even though African Americans had legally gained citizenship and the rights it guaranteed, the struggle for true equality continued in the face of continued oppression and segregation that, in effect, defined blacks as "second-class citizens." Within this context, black identity and American identity were often contradictory. At the beginning of the twentieth century, two prominent black intellectuals wrote about this contradiction: Langston Hughes (1902–1967) and W. E. B. DuBois (1868–1963). Understanding and exploring what it means to be black and American is central both to Hughes's poem "I, Too" (1925) and to "How Does It Feel To Be a Problem?" from DuBois's The Souls of Black Folk (1903).

I, Too
by Langston Hughes

I, too, sing America
I am the darker brother.
They send me to eat in the kitchen
When company comes,
But I laugh,
And eat well,
And grow strong.

Tomorrow,
I'll be at the table
When company comes
Nobody'll dare
Say to me,
"Eat in the kitchen,"
Then.

Besides,
They'll see how beautiful I am
And be ashamed—

I, too, am America.

How Does It Feel To Be a Problem?
from The Souls of Black Folk
by W. E. B. DuBois

Between me and the other world there is ever an unasked question: unasked by some through feelings of delicacy; by others through the difficulty of rightly framing it. All, nevertheless, flutter round it. They approach me in a half-hesitant sort of way, eye me curiously or compassionately, and then, instead of saying directly, How does it feel to be a problem? they say,

I know an excellent colored man in my town; or, I fought at Mechanicsville;[1] or, Do not these Southern outrages make your blood boil? At these I smile, or am interested, or reduce the boiling to a simmer, as the occasion may require. To the real question, How does it feel to be a problem? I answer seldom a word.

And yet, being a problem is a strange experience,—peculiar even for one who has never been anything else, save perhaps in babyhood and in Europe. It is in the early days of rollicking boyhood that the **revelation**[2] first bursts upon one, all in a day, as it were. I remember well when the shadow swept across me. I was a little thing, away up in the hills of New England, where the dark Housatonic winds between Hoosac and Taghkanic to the sea. In a wee wooden schoolhouse, something put it into the boys' and girls' heads to buy gorgeous visiting-cards—ten cents a package—and exchange. The exchange was merry, till one girl, a tall newcomer, refused my card,—refused it **peremptorily**,[3] with a glance. Then it dawned upon me with a certain suddenness that I was different from the others; or like, mayhap, in heart and life and longing, but shut out from their world by a vast veil. I had thereafter no desire to tear down that veil, to creep through; I held all beyond it in common contempt, and lived above it in a region of blue sky and great wandering shadows. That sky was bluest when I could beat my mates at examination-time, or beat them at a foot-race, or even beat their stringy heads. Alas, with the years all this fine contempt began to fade; for the worlds I longed for, and all their dazzling opportunities, were theirs, not mine. But they should not keep these prizes, I said; some, all, I would wrest from them. Just how I would do it I could never decide: by reading law, by healing the sick, by telling the

---

[1] Mechanicsville—site of a Civil War battle won by Union forces (June 26, 1862).

[2] **revelation**—awareness of something not previously known or realized.

[3] **peremptorily**—decisively.

wonderful tales that swam in my head,—some way. With other black boys the strife was not so fiercely sunny: their youth shrunk into tasteless **sycophancy**,[4] or into silent hatred of the pale world about them and mocking distrust of everything white; or wasted itself in a bitter cry, Why did God make me an outcast and a stranger in mine own house? The shades of the prison-house closed round about us all: walls **strait**[5] and stubborn to the whitest, but relentlessly narrow, tall, and unscalable to sons of night who must plod darkly on in resignation, or beat unavailing palms against the stone, or steadily, half hopelessly, watch the streak of blue above.

After the Egyptian and Indian, the Greek and Roman, the Teuton and Mongolian, the Negro is a sort of seventh son, born with a veil, and gifted with second-sight in this American world,—a world which yields him no true self-consciousness, but only lets him see himself through the revelation of the other world. It is a peculiar sensation, this double-consciousness, this sense of always looking at one's self through the eyes of others, of measuring one's soul by the tape of a world that looks on in amused contempt and pity. One ever feels his twoness,—an American, a Negro; two souls, two thoughts, two unreconciled strivings; two warring ideals in one dark body, whose dogged strength alone keeps it from being torn asunder.

The history of the American Negro is the history of this strife—this longing to attain self-conscious manhood, to merge his double self into a better and truer self. In this merging he wishes neither of the older selves to be lost. He would not Africanize America, for America has too much to teach the world and Africa. He would not bleach his Negro soul in a flood of white Americanism, for he knows that Negro blood has a

---

[4] **sycophancy**—flattery to gain the favor of others.
[5] **strait**—confining.

message for the world. He simply wishes to make it possible for a man to be both a Negro and an American, without being cursed and spit upon by his fellows, without having the doors of Opportunity closed roughly in his face.

QUESTIONS TO CONSIDER

1. What does Langston Hughes mean when he promises that "Tomorrow,/I'll be at the table"?

2. According to DuBois, how does being both a Negro and an American represent "two warring ideals"?

3. Who do you think presents a more positive picture of being African American, Hughes or DuBois?

4. How do Hughes and DuBois view the experience of being African American?

from

Black Boy

BY RICHARD WRIGHT

*Black Boy, the autobiography of Richard Wright (1908–1960),
was published in 1945, five years after the publication of his best-
selling novel* Native Son. *Wright had always demonstrated social
and political consciousness, and his autobiography continued that
tradition. In this selection about his childhood, spent living with his
mother and in an orphanage, Wright describes his relationship
with his absent father. He also reflects more broadly on issues of
blood ties, poverty, and race.*

After my father's desertion, my mother's **ardently**[1]
religious disposition dominated the household and I
was often taken to Sunday school where I met God's
representative in the guise of a tall, black preacher. One
Sunday my mother invited the tall, black preacher to a
dinner of fried chicken. I was happy, not because the
preacher was coming but because of the chicken. One or

---

[1] **ardently**—eagerly; passionately.

two neighbors also were invited. But no sooner had the preacher arrived than I began to resent him, for I learned at once that he, like my father, was used to having his own way. The hour for dinner came and I was wedged at the table between talking and laughing adults. In the center of the table was a huge platter of golden-brown fried chicken. I compared the bowl of soup that sat before me with the crispy chicken and decided in favor of the chicken. The others began to eat their soup, but I could not touch mine.

"Eat your soup," my mother said.

"I don't want any," I said.

"You won't get anything else until you've eaten your soup," she said.

The preacher had finished his soup and had asked that the platter of chicken be passed to him. It galled me. He smiled, cocked his head this way and that, picking out choice pieces. I forced a spoonful of soup down my throat and looked to see if my speed matched that of the preacher. It did not. There were already bare chicken bones on his plate, and he was reaching for more. I tried eating my soup faster, but it was no use; the other people were now serving themselves chicken and the platter was more than half empty. I gave up and sat staring in despair at the vanishing pieces of fried chicken.

"Eat your soup or you won't get anything," my mother warned.

I looked at her appealingly and could not answer. As piece after piece of chicken was eaten, I was unable to eat my soup at all. I grew hot with anger. The preacher was laughing and joking and the grownups were hanging on his words. My growing hate of the preacher finally became more important than God or religion and I could no longer contain myself. I leaped up from the table, knowing that I should be ashamed of what I was doing, but unable to stop, and screamed, running blindly from the room.

"That preacher's going to eat *all* the chicken!" I bawled. Mother was angry and told me that I was to have no dinner because of my bad manners.

When I awakened one morning my mother told me that we were going to see a judge who would make my father support me and my brother. An hour later all three of us were sitting in a huge crowded room. I was overwhelmed by the many faces and the voices which I could not understand. High above me was a white face which my mother told me was the face of the judge. Across the huge room sat my father, smiling confidently, looking at us. My mother warned me not to be fooled by my father's friendly manner; she told me that the judge might ask me questions, and if he did I must tell him the truth. I agreed, yet I hoped that the judge would not ask me anything.

For some reason the entire thing struck me as being useless; I felt that if my father were going to feed me, then he would have done so regardless of what a judge said to him. And I did not want my father to feed me; I was hungry, but my thoughts of food did not now center about him. I waited, growing restless, hungry. My mother gave me a dry sandwich and I munched and stared, longing to go home. Finally I heard my mother's name called; she rose and began weeping so **copiously**[2] that she could not talk for a few moments; at last she managed to say that her husband had deserted her and two children, that her children were hungry, that they stayed hungry, that she worked, that she was trying to raise them alone. Then my father was called; he came forward **jauntily**,[3] smiling. He tried to kiss my mother, but she turned away from him. I only heard one sentence of what he said.

"I'm doing all I can, Your Honor," he mumbled, grinning.

---

[2] **copiously**—plentifully, much.

[3] **jauntily**—light-heartedly.

It had been painful to sit and watch my mother crying and my father laughing and I was glad when we were outside in the sunny streets. Back at home my mother wept again and talked complainingly about the unfairness of the judge who had accepted my father's word. After the court scene, I tried to forget my father; I did not hate him; I simply did not want to think of him. Often when we were hungry my mother would beg me to go to my father's job and ask him for a dollar, a dime, a nickel. . . . But I would never consent to go. I did not want to see him.

My mother fell ill and the problem of food became an acute, daily agony. Hunger was with us always. Sometimes the neighbors would feed us or a dollar bill would come in the mail from my grandmother. It was winter and I would buy a dime's worth of coal each morning from the corner coalyard and lug it home in paper bags. For a time I remained out of school to wait upon my mother, then Granny came to visit us and I returned to school.

At night there were long, halting discussions about our going to live with Granny, but nothing came of it. Perhaps there was not enough money for railroad fare. Angered by having been hauled into court, my father now spurned us completely. I heard long, angrily whispered conversations between my mother and grandmother to the effect that "that woman ought to be killed for breaking up a home." What irked me was the ceaseless talk and no action. If someone had suggested that my father be killed, I would perhaps have become interested; if someone had suggested that his name never be mentioned, I would no doubt have agreed; if someone had suggested that we move to another city, I would have been glad. But there was only endless talk that led nowhere and I began to keep away from home as much as possible, preferring the simplicity of the streets to the worried, futile talk at home.

Finally we could no longer pay the rent for our **dingy flat;**[4] the few dollars that Granny had left us before she went home were gone. Half sick and in despair, my mother made the rounds of the charitable institutions, seeking help. She found an orphan home that agreed to assume the guidance of me and my brother provided my mother worked and made small payments. My mother hated to be separated from us, but she had no choice.

The orphan home was a two-story frame building set amid trees in a wide, green field. My mother ushered me and my brother one morning into the building and into the presence of a tall, gaunt, **mulatto**[5] woman who called herself Miss Simon. At once she took a fancy to me and I was frightened speechless; I was afraid of her the moment I saw her and my fear lasted during my entire stay in the home.

The house was crowded with children and there was always a storm of noise. The daily routine was blurred to me and I never quite grasped it. The most abiding feeling I had each day was hunger and fear. The meals were skimpy and there were only two of them. Just before we went to bed each night we were given a slice of bread smeared with molasses. The children were silent, hostile, vindictive, continuously complaining of hunger. There was an over-all atmosphere of nervousness and intrigue, of children telling tales upon others, of children being deprived of food to punish them.

The home did not have the money to check the growth of the wide stretches of grass by having it mown, so it had to be pulled by hand. Each morning after we had eaten a breakfast that seemed like no breakfast at all, an older child would lead a herd of us to the vast lawn and we would get to our knees and

---

[4] **dingy flat**—shabby apartment.

[5] **mulatto**—person of mixed black and white ancestry.

wrench the grass loose from the dirt with our fingers. At intervals Miss Simon would make a tour of inspection, examining the pile of pulled grass beside each child, scolding or praising according to the size of the pile. Many mornings I was too weak from hunger to pull the grass; I would grow dizzy and my mind would become blank and I would find myself, after an interval of unconsciousness, upon my hands and knees, my head whirling, my eyes staring in bleak astonishment at the green grass, wondering where I was, feeling that I was emerging from a dream. . . .

During the first days my mother came each night to visit me and my brother, then her visits stopped. I began to wonder if she, too, like my father, had disappeared into the unknown. I was rapidly learning to distrust everything and everybody. When my mother did come, I asked her why had she remained away so long and she told me that Miss Simon had forbidden her to visit us, that Miss Simon had said that she was spoiling us with too much attention. I begged my mother to take me away; she wept and told me to wait, that soon she would take us to Arkansas. She left and my heart sank.

Miss Simon tried to win my confidence; she asked me if I would like to be adopted by her if my mother consented and I said no. She would take me into her apartment and talk to me, but her words had no effect. Dread and distrust had already become a daily part of my being and my memory grew sharp, my senses more impressionable; I began to be aware of myself as a distinct personality striving against others. I held myself in, afraid to act or speak until I was sure of my surroundings, feeling most of the time that I was suspended over a void. My imagination soared; I dreamed of running away. Each morning I vowed that I would leave the next morning, but the next morning always found me afraid.

One day Miss Simon told me that thereafter I was to help her in the office. I ate lunch with her and, strangely, when I sat facing her at the table, my hunger vanished. The woman killed something in me. Next she called me to her desk where she sat addressing envelopes.

"Step up close to the desk," she said. "Don't be afraid."

I went and stood at her elbow. There was a wart on her chin and I stared at it.

"Now, take a blotter[6] from over there and blot each envelope after I'm through writing on it," she instructed me, pointing to a blotter that stood about a foot from my hand.

I stared and did not move or answer.

"Take the blotter," she said.

I wanted to reach for the blotter and succeeded only in twitching my arm.

"Here," she said sharply, reaching for the blotter and shoving it into my fingers.

She wrote in ink on an envelope and pushed it toward me. Holding the blotter in my hand, I stared at the envelope and could not move.

"Blot it," she said.

I could not lift my hand. I knew what she had said; I knew what she wanted me to do—and I had heard her correctly. I wanted to look at her and say something, tell her why I could not move; but my eyes were fixed upon the floor. I could not summon enough courage while she sat there looking at me to reach over the yawning space of twelve inches and blot the wet ink on the envelope.

"Blot it!" she spoke sharply.

Still I could not move or answer.

"Look at me!"

I could not lift my eyes. She reached her hand to my face and I twisted away.

"What's wrong with you?" she demanded.

---

[6] blotter—piece of absorbent paper used to dry a surface freshly written on in ink.

I began to cry and she drove me from the room. I decided that as soon as night came I would run away. The dinner bell rang and I did not go to the table, but hid in a corner of the hallway. When I heard the dishes rattling at the table, I opened the door and ran down the walk to the street. Dusk was falling. Doubt made me stop. Ought I go back? No; hunger was back there, and fear. I went on, coming to concrete sidewalks. People passed me. Where was I going? I did not know. The farther I walked the more frantic I became. In a confused and vague way I knew that I was doing more running away from than running *toward* something. I stopped. The streets seemed dangerous. The buildings were massive and dark. The moon shone and the trees loomed frighteningly. No, I could not go on. I would go back. But I had walked so far and had turned too many corners and had not kept track of the direction. Which way led back to the orphan home? I did not know. I was lost.

I stood in the middle of the sidewalk and cried. A "white" policeman came to me and I wondered if he was going to beat me. He asked me what was the matter and I told him that I was trying to find my mother. His "white" face created a new fear in me. I was remembering the tale of the "white" man who had beaten the "black" boy. A crowd gathered and I was urged to tell where I lived. Curiously, I was too full of fear to cry now. I wanted to tell the "white" face that I had run off from an orphan home and that Miss Simon ran it, but I was afraid. Finally I was taken to the police station where I was fed. I felt better. I sat in a big chair where I was surrounded by "white" policemen, but they seemed to ignore me. Through the window I could see that night had completely fallen and that lights now gleamed in the streets. I grew sleepy and dozed. My shoulder was shaken gently and I opened my eyes and looked into a "white" face of another policeman who was sitting beside me. He asked me questions in a quiet, confidential tone, and quite before I knew it he was not "white" anymore. I told him that I had run away from an orphan home and that Miss Simon ran it.

It was but a matter of minutes before I was walking alongside a policeman, heading toward the home. The policeman led me to the front gate and I saw Miss Simon waiting for me on the steps. She identified me and I was left in her charge. I begged her not to beat me, but she yanked me upstairs into an empty room and lashed me thoroughly. Sobbing, I slunk off to bed, resolved to run away again. But I was watched closely after that.

My mother was informed upon her next visit that I had tried to run away and she was terribly upset.

"Why did you do it?" she asked.

"I don't want to stay here," I told her.

"But you must," she said. "How can I work if I'm to worry about you? You must remember that you have no father. I'm doing all I can."

"I don't want to stay here," I repeated.

"Then if I take you to your father . . ."

"I don't want to stay with him either."

"But I want you to ask him for enough money for us to go to my sister's in Arkansas," she said.

Again I was faced with choices I did not like, but I finally agreed. After all, my hate for my father was not so great and urgent as my hate for the orphan home. My mother held to her idea and one night a week or so later I found myself standing in a room in a frame house. My father and a strange woman were sitting before a bright fire that blazed in a grate. My mother and I were standing about six feet away, as though we were afraid to approach them any closer.

"It's not for me," my mother was saying. "It's for your children that I'm asking you for money."

"I ain't got nothing," my father said, laughing.

"Come here, boy," the strange woman called to me.

I looked at her and did not move.

"Give him a nickel," the woman said. "He's cute."

"Come here, Richard," my father said, stretching out his hand.

I backed away, shaking my head, keeping my eyes on the fire.

"He is a cute child," the strange woman said.

"You ought to be ashamed," my mother said to the strange woman. "You're starving my children."

"Now, don't you-all fight," my father said, laughing.

"I'll take that poker and hit you!" I blurted at my father.

He looked at my mother and laughed louder.

"You told him to say that," he said.

"Don't say such things, Richard," my mother said.

"You ought to be dead," I said to the strange woman.

The woman laughed and threw her arms about my father's neck. I grew ashamed and wanted to leave.

"How can you starve your children?" my mother asked.

"Let Richard stay with me," my father said.

"Do you want to stay with your father, Richard?" my mother asked.

"No," I said.

"You'll get plenty to eat," he said.

"I'm hungry now," I told him. "But I won't stay with you."

"Aw, give the boy a nickel," the woman said.

My father ran his hand into his pocket and pulled out a nickel.

"Here, Richard," he said.

"Don't take it," my mother said.

"Don't teach him to be a fool," my father said. "Here, Richard, take it."

I looked at my mother, at the strange woman, at my father, then into the fire. I wanted to take the nickel, but I did not want to take it from my father.

"You ought to be ashamed," my mother said, weeping. "Giving your son a nickel when he's hungry. If there's a God, He'll pay you back."

"That's all I got," my father said, laughing again and returning the nickel to his pocket.

We left. I had the feeling that I had had to do with something unclean. Many times in the years after that the image of my father and the strange woman, their faces lit by the dancing flames, would surge up in my imagination so vivid and strong that I felt I could reach out and touch it; I would stare at it, feeling that it possessed some vital meaning which always eluded me.

A quarter of a century was to elapse between the time when I saw my father sitting with the strange woman and the time when I was to see him again, standing alone upon the red clay of a Mississippi plantation, a sharecropper,[7] clad in ragged overalls, holding a muddy hoe in his gnarled, veined hands—a quarter of a century during which my mind and consciousness had become so greatly and violently altered that when I tried to talk to him I realized that, though ties of blood made us kin, though I could see a shadow of my face in his face, though there was an echo of my voice in his voice, we were forever strangers, speaking a different language, living on vastly distant planes of reality. That day a quarter of a century later when I visited him on the plantation—he was standing against the sky, smiling toothlessly, his hair whitened, his body bent, his eyes glazed with dim recollection, his fearsome aspect of twenty-five years ago gone forever from him—I was overwhelmed to realize that he could never understand me or the scalding experiences that had swept me beyond his life and into an area of living that he could never know. I stood before him, poised, my mind aching as it embraced the simple nakedness of his life, feeling

---

[7] sharecropper—tenant farmer; one who works land and in return receives a portion of the crop.

how completely his soul was imprisoned by the slow flow of the seasons, by wind and rain and sun, how fastened were his memories to a crude and raw past, how chained were his actions and emotions to the direct, animalistic impulses of his withering body. . . .

From the white landowners above him there had not been handed to him a chance to learn the meaning of loyalty, of sentiment, of tradition. Joy was as unknown to him as was despair. As a creature of the earth, he endured, hearty, whole, seemingly indestructible, with no regrets and no hope. He asked easy, drawling questions about me, his other son, his wife, and he laughed, amused, when I informed him of their destinies. I forgave him and pitied him as my eyes looked past him to the unpainted wooden shack. From far beyond the horizons that bound this bleak plantation there had come to me through my living the knowledge that my father was a black peasant who had gone to the city seeking life, but who had failed in the city; a black peasant whose life had been hopelessly snarled in the city, and who had at last fled the city—that same city which had lifted me in its burning arms and borne me toward alien and undreamed-of shores of knowing.

QUESTIONS TO CONSIDER

1. Why do you think the judge accepts the father's word that he is doing all he can?

2. How would you describe the relationship between Wright and his father?

3. To what degree does Wright blame his father's shortcomings on the oppression of a society dominated by whites?

4. Why do you think the narrator stopped seeing the policeman interviewing him as "white"?

World Wars and the Black Soldier

BY THE EDITORS OF *THE CRISIS* MAGAZINE AND GRANT REYNOLDS

An important part of the efforts of the NAACP to gain equal rights for black Americans was the publication of its influential journal, The Crisis, *started in 1910. This journal was effective in providing African Americans with an outlet for their political opinions. Presented here are two editorials from* The Crisis *about the participation of blacks in World Wars I and II. These editorials examine the contradiction faced by African-American soldiers who found themselves fighting for the freedoms and rights of citizens of foreign nations while still being denied equal rights at home.*

Returning Soldiers

by the editors of *The Crisis* magazine, May 1919

We are returning from war.[1] *The Crisis* and tens of thousands of black men were drafted into a great struggle.

---

[1] war—World War I.

For bleeding France and what she means and has meant and will mean to us and humanity and against the threat of German race arrogance, we fought gladly and to the last drop of blood; for America and her highest ideals, we fought in far-off hope; for the dominant southern **oligarchy**[2] entrenched in Washington, we fought in bitter **resignation**.[3] For the America that represents and gloats in lynching, **disfranchisement**,[4] caste, brutality and devilish insult—for this, in the hateful upturning and mixing of things, we were forced by vindictive fate to fight, also.

But to-day we return! We return from the slavery of uniform which the world's madness demanded us to **don**[5] to the freedom of civil garb. We stand again to look America squarely in the face and call a spade a spade. We sing: This country of ours, despite all its better souls have done and dreamed, is yet a shameful land.

It *lynches*.

And lynching is barbarism of a degree of contemptible nastiness unparalleled in human history. Yet for fifty years we have lynched two Negroes a week, and we have kept this up right through the war.

It *disfranchises* its own citizens.

Disfranchisement is the deliberate theft and robbery of the only protection of poor against rich and black against white. The land that disfranchises its citizens and calls itself a democracy lies and knows it lies.

It encourages *ignorance*.

It has never really tried to educate the Negro. A dominant minority does not want Negroes educated. It wants servants, dogs, whores and monkeys. And when this land allows a reactionary group by its stolen political power to force as many black folk into these categories

---

[2] **oligarchy**—form of government in which power is held by only a few people.

[3] **resignation**—patient acceptance, conformity.

[4] **disfranchisement**—depriving people of their rights.

[5] **don**—put on, wear.

as it possibly can, it cries in contemptible hypocrisy: "They threaten us with **degeneracy**;[6] they cannot be educated."

It *steals* from us.

It organizes industry to cheat us. It cheats us out of our land; it cheats us out of our labor. It confiscates our savings. It reduces our wages. It raises our rent. It steals our profit. It taxes us without representation. It keeps us consistently and universally poor, and then feeds us on charity and derides our poverty.

It *insults* us.

It has organized a nation-wide and latterly a world-wide propaganda of deliberate and continuous insult and defamation of black blood wherever found. It decrees that it shall not be possible in travel nor residence, work nor play, education nor instruction for a black man to exist without tacit or open acknowledgment of his inferiority to the dirtiest white dog. And it looks upon any attempt to question or even discuss this dogma as arrogance, unwarranted assumption and treason.

This is the country to which we Soldiers of Democracy return. This is the fatherland for which we fought! But it is *our* fatherland. It was right for us to fight. The faults of *our* country are *our* faults. Under similar circumstances, we would fight again. But by the God of Heaven, we are cowards and [fools] if now that that war is over, we do not marshal every ounce of our brain and **brawn**[7] to fight a sterner, longer, more unbending battle against the forces of hell in our own land.

We *return*.
We *return from fighting*.
We *return fighting*.

---

[6] **degeneracy**—inferiority.

[7] **brawn**—physical strength.

Make way for Democracy! We saved it in France, and by the Great Jehovah, we will save it in the United States of America, or know the reason why.

What the Negro Soldier Thinks About This War[8]
by Grant Reynolds, September 1944

For the past two years and ten months I have been a Chaplain[9] on active duty with the United States Army. I have found Negro soldiers bitterly resentful of their lot in this war. My having served with Medical Troops in Virginia, Infantry Troops in Massachusetts, raw recruits at a reception center in Michigan, sick and wounded soldiers from both Negro Divisions at a hospital in Arizona, and the troops comprising a Station Complement in California, has given me a broad picture of the conditions which affect our men from coast to coast. In each instance, regardless of the geography, the net result has been the same . . . Negro soldiers are . . . tired of the treatment they are getting. This dislike cannot be attributed to the natural **antipathy**[10] of the majority of soldiers, white and black, developed out of their efforts to adjust themselves to the rigors and uncertainties of war. Now the Negro soldier is as easily adaptable as any other American soldier. I'd even go as far as to say that he is more adaptable. His lifetime of adjusting himself to the whims and inconsistencies of the American white man **substantiates**[11] this claim. His resentment then goes much deeper than this. It grows out of the un-American treatment which plagues his every day while at the same time having to listen to loud voices telling him what a great honor it is to die for his country.

---

[8] War—World War II.

[9] Chaplain—religious minister in the armed forces.

[10] **antipathy**—feeling of strong dislike; aversion.

[11] **substantiates**—proves to be true.

The Negro soldier needs no one to remind him that this is his country. He knows this. But he knows also that there is a lot of unfinished business about individual human decency that he would like to see cleared up before he becomes a corpse for any country. To deny him food when he is hungry, dignified transportation when he has to travel, a voice in choosing those who rule him, or just the most fundamental aspects of our proclaimed method of living, and then **propagandize**[12] him daily into becoming a hero for democracy, is nauseating, to say the least. As one Negro soldier asked me in this respect: "Chaplain, do the white folks who are running this war think we are fools? Or, are they a pack of [expletive] fools themselves? Excuse me, sir, for being profane, but this mess makes a man say a lot of nasty things."

Wide Experience

My tour of active duty which began in Virginia and ended in California, after periods of service in Massachusetts, Michigan, Ohio, and Arizona, has provided me the opportunity not only of observing the Negro soldier under the varied JIM-CROW conditions which make life miserable for him, but because I am a Negro too I have lived under the same conditions and shared his resentment to them. Then too it must be remembered that a chaplain who tries to do a real job does more than sermonize on Sundays. His activities extend into areas concerned with the thoughts and lives of the thousands of men he serves.

How do I know what the Negro soldier thinks? Until a few days ago I was one myself. I have lived with him in his **barracks**[13] because white officers in Virginia would not permit a colored officer to occupy quarters

---

[12] **propagandize**—urge.

[13] **barracks**—housing for soldiers.

built by the War Department for its officers. Interesting, to say the least, is a personal experience which grew out of this insult. By a sudden jolt of fate I began my military career at Camp Lee, Virginia. There I immediately discovered the South more vigorously engaged in fighting the Civil War than in training soldiers to resist Hitler. And what was obvious, though nonetheless disturbing, this war was being won . . . as far as the Negro was concerned anyway. Because of the few officers needed with my small outfit less than fifty percent of the available rooms in the officers' barracks were occupied. But there was no room for me. I was therefore assigned quarters with the enlisted men in their barracks. What did it matter that such an assignment infringed upon the freedom of Negro soldiers during their leisure moments? What did it matter how this personal embarrassment and humiliation impaired my morale? My job, it seemed, was to *build* morale, not to *have* it. Anyhow, of what importance is the condition of the Negro soldier's morale to the proper performance of his duty? But of equal importance, what did it matter that army policy prohibiting officers and enlisted men from sharing common quarters except under field conditions was deliberately ignored? The Negro soldier has learned that army policy, binding upon whites, far too often relaxes to his disadvantage. This separation of officers and enlisted men is supported on the grounds that the familiarity involved is destructive to proper discipline. There are other methods of maintaining discipline among Negro soldiers, some of which make Gestapo[14] Chief Himmler look like a rank amateur. What *did* matter in this situation was the doctrine of white supremacy which had to remain undefiled regardless of the cost. To assign a Negro officer quarters

---

[14] Gestapo—Nazi secret police notorious for its terrorism.

in an officers' barracks which housed white officers was unthinkable! Entirely ignored was the fact that this officer by virtue of his military status indicated the same willingness to die for American fair play . . . for democracy.

QUESTIONS TO CONSIDER

1. Although these two editorials were written about black participation in two different world wars, what is similar about their message?

2. What do the editors mean in the post–World War I editorial when they write, "We return. We return from fighting. We return fighting"?

3. What examples of inconsistencies in American military practice does Grant Reynolds identify in his article?

4. What reaction do you think the authors wanted from their audience?

Letter to First Lady Eleanor Roosevelt

BY CELESTINE HOBSON

Black women faced the same issues as black men concerning the contradiction between their citizenship and their unequal treatment in American society. Moreover, black women had to struggle with unequal status not only because of their race, but also because of their gender. Although women did not fight in World War II, they played an important role in the war effort, taking on industrial jobs necessary to the military that men could not fill once they went overseas to fight. Celestine Hobson, wife of a soldier, wrote to First Lady Eleanor Roosevelt in 1943 about the challenges she faced in trying to support her nation's war effort.

Chicago, Illinois
553 Lafayette Rd.
June 28, 1943

Mrs. Eleanor Roosevelt:

Dear Madame,

This letter to you is in regard of a war work defense job. I am a citizen of the United States from birth. I have a husband in the army somewhere in Africa and have two children. Ages 4 and 6. Both boys.

I am 31 years of age, and have applied at the various war industries for work. But have been turned down because I am a Negro. I would like to know from you since the world is at war, does it make any difference about the color, kind or creed and the discrimination what the war industries in Chicago have against the colored women, why they refuse to hire them. I have applications at the Studebaker Aviation Plant located at 5555 Archer Ave. in Cicero, Ill, Pullman Ship Yards in Calumet Harbor, 11010 Cottage Grove Ave., Chgo, Ill, and the Western Electric Co., 4789 W. Cermak Road also in Cicero, Ill.

I have made personal appearances at these jobs and have been turned down, merely telling me that they were filled out only to hire white girls. Since we are at war together, our men fighting for the country as well as yours, there shouldn't be any discrimination on any of these defense war jobs. We have to live as well as they do. I would like to know if there's anything you could do in regard of this matter.

I didn't finish high school. I attended Englewood High, located at 6201 Steward Ave., Chgo, Ill. I was as far a[s] 4-B[1] [and] had to quit on account of the death of father. In order to buy bonds and try to help the United

---

[1] 4-B—partly through high school, but not far enough to graduate.

States win the war I have to have a defense job making at least a decent salary to live on.

The war industries send me only $62.00 per month. With the cost of high living and food I cannot live on just that. That's why I would like to have a war industry defense job so I could at least do my part. I prefer day work on account of my children. So if you could help me get a defense job making a decent salary, approximately 45.00 or 50.00 per week I'll assure you and our fighting forces that most of the money will go in bonds for our fighting men.

Thanking Yours Very Kindly
I Remain
Mrs. Celestine Hobson

QUESTIONS TO CONSIDER

1. Why did Celestine Hobson write a letter to Eleanor Roosevelt?

2. How does Mrs. Hobson defend her right to a job?

3. What aspects of Mrs. Hobson's description of herself do you think are most important to her plea for work? Why?

Beyond Vietnam

BY MARTIN LUTHER KING, JR.

From his leadership of the Montgomery Bus Boycott in 1955 and his role in the founding of the Southern Christian Leadership Conference in 1957 until his assassination in 1968, Martin Luther King, Jr. (1929–1968) was one of the most prominent leaders of the Civil Rights movement. During his struggle for equal rights for blacks and the poor, Dr. King found it necessary to speak out against the Vietnam War. He saw similarities in the principles behind the opposition to the conflict in Vietnam and the principles of the Civil Rights movement. Here he raises the issue of the incompatibility of domestic social progress and foreign war.

Since I am a preacher by trade, I suppose it is not surprising that I have seven major reasons for bringing Vietnam into the field of my moral vision. There is at the outset a very obvious and almost **facile**[1] connection between the war in Vietnam and the struggle I, and others, have been waging in America. A few years ago

---

[1] **facile**—simple.

there was a shining moment in that struggle. It seemed as if there was a real promise of hope for the poor—both black and white—through the Poverty Program. There were experiments, hopes, new beginnings. Then came the build-up in Vietnam and I watched the program broken and **eviscerated**[2] as if it were some idle political plaything of a society gone mad on war, and I knew that America would never invest the necessary funds or energies in rehabilitation of its poor so long as adventures like Vietnam continued to draw men and skills and money like some **demonic**[3] destructive suction tube. So I was increasingly compelled to see the war as an enemy of the poor and to attack it as such.

Perhaps the more tragic recognition of reality took place when it became clear to me that the war was doing far more than devastating the hopes of the poor at home. It was sending their sons and their brothers and their husbands to fight and to die in extraordinarily high proportions relative to the rest of the population. We were taking the black young men who had been crippled by our society and sending them 8,000 miles away to guarantee liberties in Southeast Asia which they had not found in Southwest Georgia and East Harlem. So we have been repeatedly faced with the cruel irony of watching Negro and white boys on TV screens as they kill and die together for a nation that has been unable to seat them together in the same schools. So we watch them in brutal solidarity burning the huts of a poor village, but we realize that they would never live on the same block in Detroit. I could not be silent in the face of such cruel manipulation of the poor.

My third reason moves to an even deeper level of awareness, for it grows out of my experience in the

---

[2] **eviscerated**—deprived of essentials; destroyed.

[3] **demonic**—inhuman, devilish.

ghettos[4] of the north over the last three years—especially the last three summers. As I have walked among the desperate, rejected and angry young men I have told them that Molotov cocktails[5] and rifles would not solve their problems. I have tried to offer them my deepest compassion while maintaining my conviction that social change comes most meaningfully through non-violent action. But they asked—and rightly so—what about Vietnam? They asked if our own nation wasn't using massive doses of violence to solve its problems, to bring about the changes it wanted. Their questions hit home, and I knew that I could never again raise my voice against the violence of the oppressed in the ghettos without having first spoken clearly to the greatest **purveyor**[6] of violence in the world today—my own government. For the sake of those boys, for the sake of this government, for the sake of the hundreds of thousands trembling under our violence, I cannot be silent.

For those who ask the question, "Aren't you a Civil Rights leader?" and thereby mean to exclude me from the movement for peace, I have this further answer. In 1957 when a group of us formed the Southern Christian Leadership Conference, we chose as our motto: "To save the soul of America." We were convinced that we could not limit our vision to certain rights for black people, but instead affirmed the conviction that America would never be free or saved from itself unless the descendants of its slaves were loosed completely from the shackles they still wear. In a way we were agreeing with Langston Hughes, that black **bard**[7] of Harlem, who had written earlier:

---

[4] **ghettos**—impoverished, segregated neighborhoods.

[5] Molotov cocktails—crude, homemade bombs made of bottles filled with flammable liquid.

[6] **purveyor**—provider, supplier.

[7] **bard**—poet.

O, yes,
I say it plain,
America never was America to me,
And yet I swear this oath—
America will be!

Now, it should be **incandescently**[8] clear that no one who has any concern for the integrity and life of America today can ignore the present war. If America's soul becomes totally poisoned, part of the autopsy must read Vietnam. It can never be saved so long as it destroys the deepest hopes of men the world over. So it is that those of us who are yet determined that America *will* be are led down the path of protest and dissent, working for the health of our land.

As if the weight of such a commitment to the life and health of America were not enough, another burden of responsibility was placed upon me in 1964; and I cannot forget that the Nobel Prize for Peace was also a commission—a commission to work harder than I had ever worked before for "the brotherhood of man." This is a calling that takes me beyond national allegiances, but even if it were not present I would yet have to live with the meaning of my commitment to the ministry of Jesus Christ. To me the relationship of this ministry to the making of peace is so obvious that I sometimes marvel at those who ask me why I am speaking against the war. Could it be that they do not know that the good news was meant for all men—for communist and capitalist, for their children and ours, for black and for white, for revolutionary and conservative? Have they forgotten that my ministry is in obedience to the one who loved his enemies so fully that he died for them? What then can I say to the "Viet Cong" or to Castro or to Mao as a

---

[8] **incandescently**—brilliantly; extremely clear.

faithful minister of this one? Can I threaten them with death or must I not share with them my life?

Finally, as I try to **delineate**[9] for you and for myself the road that leads from Montgomery to this place I would have offered all that was most valid if I simply said that I must be true to my conviction that I share with all men the calling to be a son of the Living God. Beyond the calling of race or nation or creed is this vocation of sonship and brotherhood, and because I believe that the Father is deeply concerned especially for his suffering and helpless and outcast children, I come tonight to speak for them.

This I believe to be the privilege and the burden of all of us who deem ourselves bound by allegiances and loyalties which are broader and deeper than nationalism and which go beyond our nation's self-defined goals and positions. We are called to speak for the weak, for the voiceless, for victims of our nation and for those it calls enemy, for no document from human hands can make these humans any less our brothers.

---

[9] **delineate**—describe.

QUESTIONS TO CONSIDER

1. What are King's seven reasons for bringing Vietnam into his moral vision?

2. What allegiances are more important than allegiance to one's nation?

3. Do you think King's reasons for taking a stand against the war in Vietnam were convincing? Use examples from the selection to support your opinion.

Black Men and Public Space

BY BRENT STAPLES

*Brent Staples (1951–   ) rose from poverty to obtain a graduate
degree in journalism from the University of Chicago and a position
on the editorial board of* The New York Times. *In his book* Parallel
Time: Growing Up in Black and White, *he tells of his coming
of age and his struggles with questions of loyalty to family, class, and
race. The following essay expands on an incident recorded in* Parallel
Time. *It addresses how black men are perceived by others
in American society and continues in a tradition of Staples's work
that explores the interaction of African Americans and white society.
Staples tells of the fears aroused by stereotyping and prejudice,
and recounts his strategies for dealing with them.*

My first victim was a woman—white, well dressed,
probably in her early twenties. I came upon her late
one evening on a deserted street in Hyde Park, a relatively **affluent**[1] neighborhood in an otherwise mean,

---

[1] **affluent**—wealthy.

impoverished section of Chicago. As I swung onto the avenue behind her, there seemed to be a discreet, uninflammatory[2] distance between us. Not so. She cast back a worried glance. To her, the youngish black man—a broad six feet two inches with a beard and billowing hair, both hands shoved into the pockets of a bulky military jacket—seemed menacingly close. After a few more quick glimpses, she picked up her pace and was soon running in earnest. Within seconds she disappeared into a cross street.

That was more than a decade ago. I was twenty-two years old, a graduate student newly arrived at the University of Chicago. It was in the echo of that terrified woman's footfalls that I first began to know the **unwieldy**[3] inheritance I'd come into—the ability to alter public space in ugly ways. It was clear that she thought herself the quarry of a mugger, a rapist, or worse. Suffering a bout of insomnia, however, I was stalking sleep, not defenseless wayfarers. As a softy who is scarcely able to take a knife to a raw chicken—let alone to hold one to a person's throat—I was surprised, embarrassed, and dismayed all at once. Her flight made me feel like an accomplice in tyranny. It also made it clear that I was indistinguishable from the muggers who occasionally seeped into the area from the surrounding ghetto. That first encounter, and those that followed, signified that a vast, unnerving gulf lay between nighttime pedestrians—particularly women—and me. And I soon gathered that being perceived as dangerous is a hazard in itself. I only needed to turn a corner into a dicey[4] situation, or crowd some frightened, armed person in a foyer somewhere, or make an **errant**[5] move after being pulled over by a policeman. Where

---

[2] uninflammatory—not likely to rouse excitement, anger, or violence.

[3] **unwieldy**—hard to deal with; awkward.

[4] dicey—hazardous; chancy; risky.

[5] **errant**—straying from correct behavior.

fear and weapons meet—and they often do in urban America—there is always the possibility of death.

In that first year, my first away from my hometown, I was to become thoroughly familiar with the language of fear. At dark, shadowy intersections, I could cross in front of a car stopped at a traffic light and **elicit**[6] the thunk, thunk, thunk, thunk of the driver—black, white, male, or female—hammering down the door locks. On less traveled streets after dark, I grew accustomed to but never comfortable with people crossing to the other side of the street rather than pass me. Then there were the standard unpleasantries with policemen, doormen, bouncers, cabdrivers, and others whose business it is to screen out troublesome individuals *before* there is any nastiness.

I moved to New York nearly two years ago and I have remained an avid night walker. In central Manhattan, the near-constant crowd cover minimizes tense one-on-one street encounters. Elsewhere—in SoHo, for example, where sidewalks are narrow and tightly spaced buildings shut out the sky—things can get very taut indeed.

After dark, on the warrenlike[7] streets of Brooklyn where I live, I often see women who fear the worst from me. They seem to have set their faces on neutral, and with their purse straps strung across their chests bandolier-style,[8] they forge ahead as though bracing themselves against being tackled. I understand, of course, that the danger they perceive is not a hallucination. Women are particularly vulnerable to street violence, and young black males are drastically over-represented among the perpetrators of that violence. Yet these truths are no **solace**[9] against the kind of alienation that comes

---

[6] **elicit**—bring out; cause to be revealed.

[7] warrenlike—crowded like the area where rabbits live and breed.

[8] bandolier-style—over one shoulder and across the chest.

[9] **solace**—comfort; consolation.

of being ever the suspect, a fearsome entity with whom pedestrians avoid making eye contact.

It is not altogether clear to me how I reached the ripe old age of twenty-two without being conscious of the lethality[10] nighttime pedestrians attributed to me. Perhaps it was because in Chester, Pennsylvania, the small, angry industrial town where I came of age in the 1960s, I was scarcely noticeable against a backdrop of gang warfare, street knifings, and murders. I grew up one of the good boys, had perhaps a half-dozen fistfights. In retrospect, my shyness of combat has clear sources.

As a boy, I saw countless tough guys locked away; I have since buried several, too. They were babies, really—a teenage cousin, a brother of twenty-two, a childhood friend in his mid-twenties—all gone down in episodes of **bravado**[11] played out in the streets. I came to doubt the virtues of intimidation early on. I chose, perhaps unconsciously, to remain a shadow—timid, but a survivor.

The fearsomeness mistakenly attributed to me in public places often has a perilous flavor. The most frightening of these confusions occurred in the later 1970s and early 1980s, when I worked as a journalist in Chicago. One day, rushing into the office of a magazine I was writing for with a deadline story in hand, I was mistaken for a burglar. The office manager called security and, with an ad hoc posse,[12] pursued me through the **labyrinthine**[13] halls, nearly to my editor's door. I had no way of proving who I was. I could only move briskly toward the company of someone who knew me.

---

[10] lethality—ability to cause death.

[11] **bravado**—pretended courage or defiant confidence when there is really little or none.

[12] ad hoc posse—a group of armed men picked for a single purpose.

[13] **labyrinthine**—intricate; complicated like a labyrinth, an elaborate maze.

Another time I was on assignment for a local paper and killing time before an interview. I entered a jewelry store on the city's affluent Near North Side. The proprietor excused herself and returned with an enormous red Doberman pinscher straining at the end of a leash. She stood, the dog extended toward me, silent to my questions, her eyes bulging nearly out of her head. I took a **cursory**[14] look around, nodded, and bade her good night.

Relatively speaking, however, I never fared as badly as another black male journalist. He went to nearby Waukegan, Illinois, a couple of summers ago to work on a story about a murderer who was born there. Mistaking the reporter for the killer, police officers hauled him from his car at gunpoint and but for his press credentials would probably have tried to book him. Such episodes are not uncommon. Black men trade tales like this all the time.

Over the years, I learned to smother the rage I felt at so often being taken for a criminal. Not to do so would surely have led to madness. I now take precautions to make myself less threatening. I move about with care, particularly late in the evening. I give a wide berth[15] to nervous people on subway platforms during the wee hours, particularly when I have exchanged business clothes for jeans. If I happen to be entering a building behind some people who appear **skittish**,[16] I may walk by, letting them clear the lobby before I return, so as not to seem to be following them. I have been calm and extremely congenial on those rare occasions when I've been pulled over by the police.

---

[14] **cursory**—hasty; performed rapidly with little attention to detail.

[15] wide berth—large space or area.

[16] **skittish**—easily frightened; jumpy.

And on late-evening **constitutionals**[17] I employ what has proved to be an excellent tension-reducing measure: I whistle melodies from Beethoven and Vivaldi and the more popular classical composers. Even steely New Yorkers hunching toward nighttime destinations seem to relax, and occasionally they even join in the tune. Virtually everybody seems to sense that a mugger wouldn't be warbling bright, sunny selections from Vivaldi's *Four Seasons*. It is my equivalent of the cowbell that hikers wear when they know they are in bear country.

---

[17] **constitutionals**—walks taken for one's health.

QUESTIONS TO CONSIDER

1. What experiences does Staples describe that tell us about how black men are perceived in American society? What do these experiences tell us?

2. Staples begins his essay with the line, "My first victim was a woman—white, well-dressed, probably in her early twenties." Why does he use the word *victim*?

3. Do you approve of the ways Staples chooses to deal with the fears of others? Why or why not?

4. In what ways is Staples's problem a problem for everyone? What could be done to eliminate the problem?

Keep Your Eyes on the Prize

Slaves relied on spirituals for inspiration as they endured slavery. Participants in the Civil Rights movement of the 1950s and 1960s, whose nonviolent protests repeatedly faced violent reaction and political resistance from white Southerners, also drew strength from spirituals in their pursuit of social progress and equality. The freedom songs of the movement originated from early slave spirituals and work and protest songs of the 1930s and 1940s. They continued a tradition that linked the musical expression of faith with the struggle for freedom and equality. "Keep Your Eyes on the Prize" is one of many songs from a canon that also includes "Free at Last" and "We Shall Overcome."

Paul and Silas[1] bound in jail,
Had no money for to go their bail.
Keep your eyes on the prize,
Hold on, hold on.
  Hold on, hold on.
Keep your eyes on the prize,
  Hold on, hold on.

Paul and Silas begin to shout,
The jail door open and they walked out.
Keep your eyes on the prize,
Hold on, hold on.

Freedom's name is mighty sweet,
Soon one day we're gonna meet.
Keep your eyes on the prize,
Hold on, hold on.

Got my hand on the Gospel plow,
I wouldn't take nothing for my journey now.
Keep your eyes on the prize,
Hold on, hold on.

The only chain that a man can stand,
Is that chain of hand in hand.
Keep your eyes on the prize,
Hold on, hold on.

The only thing that we did wrong,
Stayed in the wilderness a day too long.
Keep your eyes on the prize,
Hold on, hold on.

---

[1] Paul and Silas—the Apostle Paul and his companion Silas, who were imprisoned during their efforts to spread Christianity.

But the one thing we did right,
Was the day we started to fight.
Keep your eyes on the prize,
Hold on, hold on.

We're gonna board that big Greyhound,[2]
Carryin' love from town to town.
Keep your eyes on the prize,
Hold on, hold on.

We've met jail and violence too,
But God's love has seen us through.
Keep your eyes on the prize,
Hold on, hold on.

Haven't been to Heaven but I've been told,
Streets up there are paved with gold.
Keep your eyes on the prize,
Hold on, hold on.

---

[2] Greyhound—bus.

QUESTIONS TO CONSIDER

1. What is the "prize"?

2. What is the significance of the lines, "The only chain that a man can stand,/is that chain of hand in hand"?

3. What aspects of this song do you think participants in the Civil Rights movement would have found inspirational?

ACKNOWLEDGEMENTS

22 From *Juneteenth* by Ralph Ellison. Copyright © 1999 by Fanny Ellison. Reprinted by permission of Random House, Inc.

41 "The Creation" from *God's Trombones* by James Weldon Johnson. Copyright 1927 The Viking Press, Inc., renewed by Grace Nail Johnson. Used by permission of Viking Penguin, a division of Penguin Putnam.

44 "Jubilee," by Sabah As-Sabah. Reprinted by permission from *In The Tradition: An Anthology of Young Black Writers* edited by Kevin Powell and Ras Baraka (Harlem River Press: 1992).

64 "Second-Hand Man," from *Fifth Sunday*, Callaloo Fiction Series. Copyright 1985 by Rita Dove. Reprinted by permission of the author.

73 From *The Wedding* by Dorothy West. Copyright © 1995 by Dorothy West. Used by permission of Doubleday, a division of Random House, Inc.

86 "Beverly Hills, Chicago" from *Blacks* by Gwendolyn Brooks. (Chicago: Third World Press, 1991)

87 "We Real Cool," from *Blacks* by Gwendolyn Brooks. (Chicago: Third World Press, 1991)

89 "Nikki-Rosa" from *Black Feeling, Black Talk, Black Judgment* by Nikki Giovanni. Copyright © 1968, 1970 by Nikki Giovanni. By permission of William Morrow and Company, Inc.

91 From *Jazz* by Toni Morrison, Alfred A. Knopf, 1992. Reprinted by permission of International Creative Management, Inc.

100 "Hip Hop Bop," by Jabari Asim. Reprinted by permission of Jabari Asim.

101 "Jazzoetry" from *The Last Poets: Vibes from the Scribes, Selected Poems*, by Jalal Nuriddin and Suliaman El Hadi. Permission granted by the publisher, Africa World Press, Inc. All rights reserved.

116 From *Notes of A Native Son* by James Baldwin. Copyright © 1955, renewed 1983, by James Baldwin. Reprinted by permission of Beacon Press, Boston.

125 "Why I Like Contry Music" from *Elbow Room* by James Alan McPherson, 1977, Atlantic-Monthly Press, Little Brown. Reprinted by permission of the author.

135 "Beauty: When the Other Dancer Is the Self" from *In Search of Our Mothers' Gardens: Womanist Prose,* copyright © 1983 by Alice Walker, reprinted by permission of Harcourt, Inc.

146 From *Blue As The Lake* by Robert Stepto. Copyright © 1998 by Robert B. Stepto. Reprinted by permission of Beacon Press, Boston.

162 From *Unafraid of the Dark* by Rosemary L. Bray. Copyright © 1998 by Rosemary L. Bray. Reprinted by permission of Random House, Inc.

174 From *Caucasia* by Danzy Senna, copyright © 1998 by Danzy Senna. Used by permission of Riverhead Books, a division of Penguin Putnam, Inc.

197 "I, Too" from *Collected Poems* by Langston Hughes. Copyright © 1994 by the Estate of Langston Hughes. Reprinted by permission of Alfred A. Knopf Inc.

201 From *Black Boy* by Richard Wright. Copyright, 1937, 1942, 1944, 1945 by Richard Wright. Copyright renewed 1973 by Ellen Wright. Reprinted by permission of HarperCollins Publishers, Inc.

216 "What the Negro Soldier Thinks About This War," by Grant Reynolds from *The Crisis Magazine,* September 1944. The editor wishes to thank The Crisis Publishing Co., Inc., the publisher of the magazine of the National Association for the Advancement of Colored People, for authorizing the use of this work.

220 "Letter to Eleanor Roosevelt" 28 June 1943; Creator—Celestine Hobson. Reprinted by permission of Chicago Historical Society.

223 "Beyond Vietnam" by Martin Luther King, Jr. Reprinted by arrangement with The Heirs to the Estate of Martin Luther King, Jr., c/o Writers House, Inc. as agent for the proprietor. Copyright 1967 by Martin Luther King, Jr., copyright renewed 1995 by The Estate of Martin Luther King, Jr.

228 "Black Men and Public Space" by Brent Staples. Reprinted by permission of the author.

Photo Research Diane Hamilton

Photos 60–61, 62 *bottom,* **187, 188, 194** *top* AP/Wide World Photo. **62, 185, 191** © Bettmann/CORBIS.

All other photos courtesy of the Library of Congress and the National Archives.

Every effort has been made to secure complete rights and permissions for each selection presented herein. Updated acknowledgements, if needed, will appear in subsequent printings.

Index